ON THE USES

OF MILITARY POWER

IN THE

NUCLEAR AGE

Published for the Princeton Center of International Studies.
A list of other Center publications appears at the back of the book.

ON THE USES

OF MILITARY POWER

IN THE

NUCLEAR AGE

BY KLAUS KNORR

PRINCETON, NEW JERSEY

PRINCETON UNIVERSITY PRESS

1966

Publication of this book has been aided by
the Whitney Darrow Publication Reserve Fund
of Princeton University Press

Printed in the United States of America
by Princeton University Press
Princeton, New Jersey

PREFACE

THE FOLLOWING ESSAY grew out of thoughts first developed in a lecture delivered at the SANDIA Corporation in Albuquerque, New Mexico, in June 1965. The essay is not concerned with policy, although the analysis and tentative conclusions presented would seem to be germane to the making of policy; and it is not specially concerned with the United States, even though it deals with a range of problems importantly confronting the United States as well as other nations. Instead, this essay examines trends discernible in the nature of military conflict, in political attitudes toward war as a method for settling disputes, and hence trends affecting the place of military power in international relations and the utility of war and armed forces. These conditions, and the changes they display, have a major bearing on the structure and functioning of the international systems.

This book is meant to contribute to an understanding of these matters. It does not offer a general theory of military power. Such a theory, it seems to me, is not yet within our reach. The relevant conceptual apparatus now in use is still very confused and quite inadequate to the task of comprehending reality in anything approaching depth. Such empirical work as has been done—much of it published in the *Journal of Conflict Resolution*—is a mere beginning and, though promising in parts, shows the difficulty of obtaining good data. However, if our grasp of the problems of war and military power is to become firmer, if there is to be more clarity and refinement in our understanding of these phenomena, empirical work utilizing a variety of methods must go hand in hand with attempts to achieve conceptual sophistication. A focus on middle-level theory, as much as possible based on empirical research, might well be the best strategy.

As explained more fully in Chapter I, many of my propositions lack a substantial underpinning fashioned from the sort of material that the painstaking research of many scholars must and, it is hoped, will eventually provide. These materials are not now on hand. And yet I persuaded myself that the attempt at viewing so many aspects of reality in their interconnectedness should not wait until more groundwork has been done. The sorts of groundwork that are needed can be specified only when all the dimensions of the required structure are sketched out.

Since I was forced to cope with so many aspects of international, and indeed human, affairs, my task was suited to profit from the advice and criticism of many scholars commanding a wide variety of expertise. I learned much from the existing literature but, since this manuscript was virtually finished in October 1965, I was unable to consult works that have appeared since, such as Stanley Hoffmann's *The State of War*. I am greatly indebted to many readers of my drafts, although I alone am responsible for the final product, and this not in the least because I was often unable to follow the advice I received. My associates in the Center of International Studies in 1964-1965, or in the present academic year, who read either my original lecture or an earlier draft of this book, are: Cyril E. Black, Harry Eckstein, Richard A. Falk, Mohammed Guessous, Norman Gibbs, Manfred Halpern, Merle Kling, Gregory Massell, Mancur Olson, Jr., Thornton Read, Harold Sprout, Harvey Waterman, Ann Ruth Willner, and Oran Young. I also benefited from the criticism of William

Janeway, an undergraduate student who was in my graduate seminar on "Military Aspects of International Affairs" in the Spring term of 1965. Other scholars who read my first paper, and helped me with critical advice, were Bernard Brodie (The RAND Corporation), W. T. R. Fox (Columbia), Morton H. Halperin (Harvard), Arno Mayer (Princeton), Oskar Morgenstern (Princeton), Jeremy Stone (Harvard), Howard T. Stump (SANDIA Corporation), and Fred Wyle (then in the Department of State). As I have had occasion to do so many times before, I must thank Jean MacLachlan for skillfully editing the manuscript, and Jane McDowall not only for typing the manuscript but also for protecting me from my environment enough to give me the time for writing it.

Princeton, New Jersey
October 1965

CONTENTS

ON THE USES

OF MILITARY POWER

IN THE

NUCLEAR AGE

CHAPTER I

THE PROBLEM AND

ITS PROBLEMS

HAS THERE BEEN an appreciable change, since World War II, in the values derived by nation-states from the development and use of national military power? To raise this question is surely appropriate at a time when the leaders of many states, including the United States and the Soviet Union, have flatly declared that war—at least nuclear war—has ceased to be a rational instrument of policy, when official declarations on matters of arms control and disarmament have become frequent, and when, indeed, arms control and disarmament have become the subject not only of a large and growing literature on their principles, techniques, and practicality, but also of numerous and protracted conferences among governments.

These conferences have so far yielded few tangible results, an outcome which seems to reflect the difficulties of designing agreements sure to increase rather than diminish the security of the parties, and especially of proceeding safely, in terms of security, from armament to disarmament. These difficulties may well inspire skepticism or pessimism even in those genuinely attracted to disarmament as a possible approach to enhanced security. Nevertheless, the attraction persists. And even if it were true, as some observers allege, that the United States and the Soviet Union are not seriously interested in general and complete disarmament, to which their governments proclaim themselves to be in principle committed, and that both are cynically pretending to such an interest only in order to compete for the favors of world public opinion, the need for making this pretense would testify to the importance of arms control and disarmament as live ideas capable of agitating a good many people.

It may also be contended that the disarmament idea was already prevalent in the 1920's and early 1930's without provoking much implementing action, and without preventing the policies that led to World War II. But this failure to produce practical results evidently has not caused the idea to be discarded as so much hypocrisy and illusion. It is continuing to work on many minds, and the literature produced by this engrossment since World War II is very much larger in volume and richer in thought than that which appeared following World War I. To those convinced of the need for general and complete disarmament, national military power has obviously come to represent a net disutility to their own nation and to mankind as a whole. They are, to be sure, a small if vociferous minority in any country.

Yet there are many more in many countries who, though less sure and less committed, have grave doubts and gnawing anxieties about the present foundations of security, and many scholarly students of international affairs have come to gloomy conclusions on the subject. Quincy Wright, for instance, repeating the dictum of many statesmen, finds that modern weapons have "made war too dangerous for nuclear powers to use as an instrument of policy";[1] and Inis Claude, believing that mankind "stands in grave danger of irreparable self-mutilation or substantial self-destruction," thinks of this predicament as the "crucial fact about the human situa-

[1] Quincy Wright, *A Study of War*, 2nd ed., Chicago: University of Chicago Press, 1965, p. 1519.

tion in the mid-twentieth century. . . ."[2] It seems indeed fair to conclude that mankind is in a quandary about the utility of military power organized and regulated on the basis of national sovereignty.

But though it is hardly farfetched to inquire into the changing utility of national military power, the question of what happened to it is not easy to answer. The difficulties involved, which are spelled out in the following pages, should not be allowed to be daunting and to inhibit the beginning of systematic analysis. Political leaders cannot and do not ignore these questions even though they are spared the necessity of propounding formal answers; and they are entitled to any knowledge, however fragmentary and uncertain, and to any judgment, no matter how risky, that can be brought to bear on the subject. And the fact is that a great deal can be said with confidence about its validity, or at least with the expectation that further analysis will be encouraged and that our understanding of the problem will benefit from cumulative elucidation. But it would be fatal to ignore the difficulties encountered in any approach to the problem.

There are four notable obstacles. For one thing, a *general* answer might prove difficult to make convincing, or be so flat as to arouse little interest. To touch interest one has to go into specifics. If one encounters the statement that military power has lost in value, one is prompted to ask: How much has it lost in utility, if there has been any loss at all? And utility for what purpose? And to whom? And under what, if not all, circumstances? And military power in all its forms and modes of employment, or only in some? It is through such proliferation of questions—reflecting the richly conditional

[2] Inis L. Claude, *Power and International Relations*, New York: Random House, 1962, p. 3.

nature of the problem—that we may approach reality. There are clearly more such questions than can be accommodated in this essay and by its author. All I can hope to do is examine some of them and stimulate others to do likewise.

A second difficulty arises from the vast complexity of the subject matter. It demands attention to far more aspects of human behavior, many only dimly understood, than any one author is competent to exercise. Thus, part of the problem concerns uses of military power, and their consequences, regarding which there is no experience to draw on. Since Hiroshima and Nagasaki no nuclear weapon has been fired in war, and no major military powers have been directly at war with one another. About such contingencies we can only speculate. But even regarding the present and past, social scientists and historians have not assembled the information, and thereby produced the supporting literature, that would permit many aspects of the problem to be illuminated in their relationship and put into proper perspective. What have been the attitudes of various classes of people in various countries toward military power and war in the course of the nineteenth century and the twentieth? Have there been significant shifts in these attitudes and in related behavior? As suggested above, is there today a keener interest in the possibility of arms control and disarmament than there was in the 1920's? In which ways has the legitimacy of war changed over time, and how are the attitudes relevant to this legitimacy distributed at this time? How did it come about that Frenchmen, Germans, Italians, and Englishmen cannot at present conceive of waging war against one another, even though they have done so with appalling frequency for many hundreds of years, and until very recently? Most of these questions, and many more, are capable of being subjected to empirical research. Most of this research, however, has not been undertaken so far. And yet I cannot ignore at least some of these questions and hence am forced more often than not to offer unsupported opinion and guesswork. This procedure necessarily puts an excessive burden on my limited knowledge and judgment. It is only fair that my suggestions and assertions be questioned; and it is hoped that others will be stimulated to do the spade-work on which confident answers must eventually rest.

Third, the utility of military power—to a nation or government—evidently may be derived from a vast range of values and interests. Many of these do not, at least directly, involve interstate relations. Thus, governments may value military forces for the purpose of internal control and security rather than international employment. The maintenance of military forces may be to the advantage of particular career and business interests, or lend support to national economic prosperity and growth. In a good many countries, the armed services are often called upon to perform such non-military tasks as harvesting crops and fighting floods and forest fires. The armed forces may be cherished as a repository of past military glory, regarded as a symbol of national unity, and appreciated as part of the system of education and social integration and mobilization. Indeed, if the newly established states have acquired armies, navies, and air forces—sometimes of a kind and size hardly justified by international exigencies—their governments may have done so as part of their business of building a nation, of promoting national self-identity, or —by displaying the traditional appurtenances of the nation-state—they may simply have been satisfying their craving for status and self-respect.

Indubitably, such political, economic, and psychological benefits account for much of the utility that nations derive from the stuff of military power and, in many countries, for the size and kind of forces presently in commission. This book is not, however, essentially concerned with these kinds of values, important as they certainly are. On the whole, it is limited to exploring the value of national military power as an instrument of foreign policy. It focuses on the international use and usefulness of military forces and on the maintenance of such forces only to the extent that they serve this purpose. To the extent that we are concerned with the international effects of military power, we are interested in the utility of international war, in the utility of explicit military threats, and in the utility derived from the mere possession of military forces that—on account of the implicit or latent threat embodied in them—may affect the behavior of governments.

The fourth and crucial difficulty—and one to be faced squarely—is that, speak though we may of the utility of military power, we are unable to measure it. Utility is a matter of perception and values. It is essentially subjective, and this fact precludes computation and prevents comparison between countries and over time. We are unable to say whether the leaders of the Soviet Union derive more utility from their country's military power than do the leaders of Sweden or Senegal, or whether British leaders find British forces more or less useful in 1965 than their predecessors did in 1930.

However, even though we are unable to quantify and rigorously compare, the concept of utility offers an analytical advantage. It helps us to give the problem some conceptual structure. And aided by this structure, we are able to observe some relevant changes in conditions that, by themselves, *tend* to diminish or increase the value of national military power; and we may observe changes in the use of military power that suggest hypotheses about changes in its utility.

A CONCEPTUAL FORMULA

We may begin with a simple formula, even though this is not to suggest that the realities involved are capable of quantification.

$$U = V - C = (V_1 + V_2 + \dots V_n) - (C_1 + C_2 + \dots C_n)$$

The utility (U) which a nation, or its leaders, derives from military power—that is, from its maintenance and use—depends on the satisfaction of certain values (V) and the accrual of certain costs (C). Utility depends on the difference between aggregate values and aggregate costs.

It is also clear that there are various kinds of values ($V_1, V_2, \dots V_n$) and various kinds of costs ($C_1, C_2, \dots C_n$), even if we disregard the values excluded on the previous page. I will not offer an exhaustive typology of values or costs, but wish to indicate their variety and range. Study of the behavior of states throughout recorded history reveals a large variety of particular foreign-policy purposes on behalf of which military power has been employed. Most, if not all, of these purposes can be reduced to two classes: defensive or non-acquisitive goals, and offensive or acquisitive goals.

Foremost among defensive goals has been the preservation of physical security from external aggression since, under the past and present international order, territorial integrity has been, and still is, the indispensable basis for a high degree of self-determination, if not for sheer survival. Defensive goals may include two further lines of interest. One line involves the undisturbed satisfaction of established interests abroad that can be threatened, and that are capable of being defended by military means. These interests may include international trade, foreign investments, access to and free passage through the sea, the protection of nationals abroad, and such intangibles as the preservation of international respect, honor, and prestige. The other line follows from considerations of the international balance of power—that is, opposition to the expanding military might of an aggressive and growing power, or powers, by means of defensive alliances and possibly even preventive war. In brief, defensive goals involve the protection of various assets and advantages that are part of the *status quo*.

Historically foremost among offensive goals has been the conquest, for purposes of possession or control, of territory—whether valued for its population, economic resources, or military advantage. In addition, military power has been employed for the acquisition of various other assets, including foreign respect and prestige. In short, offensive goals involve the acquisition of various assets and advantages in a way that, through the employment of military power, revises the international *status quo*. In either case, whether used defensively or offensively, military power lends a measure of international freedom of action of the state involved.*

---

* This classification is not concerned with the deep, complex, and ill-understood motivations that make governments pursue either offensive or defensive goals. Several theorists maintain that military aggression is only superficially related to the assets indicated above, and is primarily prompted by basic human drives that are unconscious and uncontrollable. Thus, one historian speculates that "aggressiveness is somehow related to the character of power itself," that "a certain position of power . . . will . . . in fact produce a corrupting effect," and he quotes Acton to the effect that "There is one thing which has caused more strife in the world than race or religion or the conflict of political ideas; and that is the tendency of power as such to expand indefinitely, transcending all barriers at home and abroad, until it is met by a force superior to it."

The costs of developing, maintaining, and employing military power are likewise of considerable variety. By "costs" we mean not just financial burdens but all reductions in valued things, and all increases in things valued negatively. The costs of developing and maintaining national military power are direct and indirect, manifest and latent. There always are the financial or economic costs—that is to say, the allocation to the military sector of society of various economic resources: manpower, skills, raw materials, land, and capital. The real economic costs are the uses of these resources for other purposes—private and public consumption and investment—that are foregone when they are expended on military efforts. The foregone uses represent a value loss. If a nation maintains any system of compulsory military service, there is the additional cost—if the experience of military service is so valued—of regimentation, that is, the reduced self-direction of drafted individuals and, possibly, the burdens imposed on their families. The costs increase greatly once military power is used in war or in threats of war. In the event of war, the "peacetime" costs just described are apt to rise as military expenditure mounts and military manpower is expanded. In addition, there is of course the increased personal insecurity of soldiers and, possibly, civilians;

(Herbert Butterfield, *Christianity, Diplomacy and War*, London: Epworth Press, 1953, pp. 56f.)

There is also Schumpeter's theory, according to which war and conquest may represent the "objectless" imperialism of a state that serves the satisfaction of a warrior or other militant organization, demanding and compelling its use regardless of specific objectives. (Cf. Joseph A. Schumpeter, *Imperialism and Social Classes*, New York: Augustus Kelley, 1951, p. 408.) This theory seems to refer to the desire of nations and organizations to "act out their character." (Cf. Karl W. Deutsch, *The Nerves of Government*, New York: Free Press, 1963, p. 111.) Character may be peaceful or bellicose, and power means the ability to act it out.

the destruction of life and property; and the risk of defeat with all its possible consequences.

Following war, individuals, families, and society may suffer not only from the possible consequences of defeat, and from postponed financial payment for the war effort, but also from the fact that many families have lost one or more valued members, and that a proportion of soldiers (and perhaps civilians as well) have survived as physical or psychological cripples. In the event the war was aggressive in origin and conduct, the nation involved may also endure political disadvantages in terms of foreign distrust, hatred, and revengefulness; and the victorious nation that has emerged with greatly increased power may in any case face the preparations of foreign nations to balance and possibly reduce its power. If a nation precipitated and waged war aggressively, it may also bear moral costs in terms of diminished self-respect to the extent it is aware of any "guilt." The costs of military threats involve the risks either of having one's bluff called—which would be tantamount to a loss of military power and other international assets such as prestige—or of bearing the various costs of war. In general, risks are an important class of costs. The risk that a certain kind of cost may be incurred will be experienced in terms of a subjective probability that something of value will be lost or diminished.

It is clear from our formula that the utility of war and of military power is subject to change. Students of history have indeed concluded that this is the case.[3] Such changes will occur if there are shifts, uncompensated by shifts in the opposite direction, in the values derived from, or the costs incurred by, the maintenance and use of national military power. Thus, the value or the cost

[3] Quincy Wright, *A Study of War*, 1st ed., Chicago: University of Chicago Press, 1942, II, pp. 853ff.

side may undergo changes. On the value side, there may occur a diminution or augmentation of the valued objects for the attainment of which military power can be applied; or these objects may rise or fall in value. On the cost side, there may occur a reduction or enlargement of costs in terms of kind or magnitude; or their costs may become subjectively more or less appreciated in terms of magnitude.

At any one time, variations in values and costs expected from the maintenance and use of military power in part account for differences among nations in their attitudes toward maintaining military power, and toward its aggressive or defensive employment. Some nations are readier than others to accumulate and exploit military power because they entertain higher expectations of gain from doing so. The utility they expect is comparatively large. And as is the case with the differing interest of individuals in acquiring power within any political community,[4] of two states, state A may expect greater gain from military power than B because it appears less costly to develop and use, or because the expected outcome of its use appears more valuable to it than to B. The costs may appear lower, for example, because the economic opportunity costs are lower, perhaps because A is rich and B is poor, or because A is unbothered by relevant moral compunctions. The expected gains may appear higher for A than for B because, for example, A has a larger war potential and hence a lesser need to fear the test of its power and ultimate defeat, or because it values conquest more than B. In other words, A might expect different results than B, feel more confident about the outcome, or apply different values to the appraisal of possible outcomes. How-

[4] Cf. Robert A. Dahl, *Modern Political Analysis*, Englewood Cliffs, N.J.: Prentice-Hall, 1964, p. 69.

ever, this essay is less interested in such differences as might exist between nations at any one time than in changes in the utility of military power over time. Such changes affect the entire system of nation-states and, therefore, impinge more or less on all nations, their behavior, and their relations.

There is one further condition, or complex of conditions, that bears on the utility of military power and its employment. The gains in value obtainable through the use of national military power may sometimes be procured also by the employment of non-military means, both coercive and non-coercive; that is, there are other bases of international influence than military power. Nations may impose or threaten to impose on one another such penalties as adverse propaganda, righteous denunciations, recall of ambassadors, suspension of diplomatic relations, economic pressures (including the curtailment or termination of foreign aid, and the confiscation of foreign economic assets within their domain), withdrawal from alliances, and so on. Similarly, nations may offer rewards such as alliance, various economic benefits, exchange of friendly official visits, and the like.

These various forms of international influence are not, to be sure, fully interchangeable. For many purposes, and in many situations, the non-military means are only a partial substitute for military power; and for some purposes, and in some situations (e.g., defense against military attack), they may be no substitute at all. On the other hand, though some of these other means of influence are not used without costs (e.g., economic aid or the conclusion of an alliance), their total costs may fall far short of the costs of military power and its use. The non-military means of international influence have their own utility:

$$U = (V_a + V_b + \ldots V_n) - (C_a + C_b + \ldots C_n)$$

As in the case of military power, this utility is subject to change as values and costs increase or decline. To the extent that their utility changes, and to the extent that non-military means are a substitute for military power, the use of the latter may look more or less advantageous than before, and the utility of military power will tend to rise or fall correspondingly.

Nor is the problem only a matter of substituting one means for another. In the pursuit of foreign-policy objectives, statesmen usually employ a combination of different means, both military and non-military. They design and use a "power package" in which the various means of influence are proportioned and concerted to best effect. As in all human affairs, force of habit is a powerful agent and stereotype responses—reflecting some old and, in a dynamically changing world, frequently obsolete or obsolescent wisdom—will often shape the design. But to the extent that statesmen are rational, observant, and calculating, and the power package is flexible in composition, they will adjust the components in response to the changing utilities of all the useful means on hand. Here again, at any one time nation-states may differ not only in the pragmatic ingenuity of their leaders, but also in the availability and utility of the means at their disposal, and in their susceptibility to various means employed by other states. But there may also occur changes in relative utilities throughout the international system. If this happens and the utility of military power declines, or the utility of non-military means rises, governments will tend to increase reliance on the non-military instruments of policy; and they will tend to take the opposite tack if utility changes are reversed. In fact, the utility of military power depends to some extent on the utility of non-military means of international influence.

Indeed, we strongly suspect that, during the past two decades, some means of international influence other than military power have—relative to the exertion of military strength—appreciated in value. Offers of economic aid, particularly in the form of international loans and gifts, had considerable currency during the immediate period following World War II, when many war-ravaged communities were in desperate need of resources permitting speedy recovery. But even now that this transitory condition has disappeared, the extension of economic advantages exerts considerable pulling power. As an instrument of statecraft, its usability has gained from the vast additions to national incomes experienced by most highly developed countries; and its capacity for affording influence has benefited from the increased desire of the poorer communities to advance economically and, in a good many cases, to live beyond their means. As a result of the copious and continuing increase in the network and volume of international communications, and the growing ability of governments and elites the world over to emit and receive political messages, we also believe that the power of well-formulated and well-directed information and propaganda has increased substantially. This augmented availability and impact of non-military means of international influence should not, of course, be exaggerated. The extent to which they can supplement the exertion of military power, let alone replace it altogether, is clearly limited. Nonetheless, their rise has tended to curtail the utility of military power for a range of foreign-policy purposes, and may well have made the appeal to force entirely irrelevant in some cases.

CHAPTER II

THE INTERNATIONAL PURPOSES

OF MILITARY POWER

A s REPORTED IN Chapter I, statesmen and scholars have maintained that in recent years or decades the utility of military power—particularly nuclear military power—as an instrument of policy has declined, if not slumped dramatically. And, as explained in the theoretical introduction, such a decline—if, and to the extent that, it has actually taken place and did not occur through the rising influence of non-military means—must have resulted from a lessened expectation of gains to be secured by means of such power or from increased costs in its use. In this chapter we will discuss the advantages of military power and inquire into any changes in national expectations about these advantages. In order to do so, we must first clarify the nature of power and its place in the international system.

NATURE AND PURPOSES OF INTERNATIONAL POWER

Power is a form of influence and, like other forms of influence, it has several dimensions. Power is coercive influence based on the threat of value deprivation or penalties. Such penalties may take several forms, one of them being military. Military power is ultimately the power to destroy and kill, or to occupy and control, and hence to coerce. In the international system, military power—like other forms of influence—is a relation among states that permits one government to induce another to behave in a way which the latter would not have chosen freely. Military power thus permits a degree of control over the environment.

Military power results, in large part, from military force, but the two are completely different phenomena— a difference that is often overlooked in practice as well as theory. Regiments, naval vessels, rockets, and nuclear bombs are concrete things. They are instruments for generating military power. But military power, like all power and influence, is relational. If we were to suppose that infantry divisions were the only kind of military force, country A with five divisions might have military power over country B with two divisions, but only if there were no offsetting differences in other properties than numbers (e.g., generalship, valor, equipment), if A were physically able to bring its forces to bear on B, and if A were willing to commit these forces against B. A nation's military power is obviously relative to that of other powers, but it is also sensitive to other factors such as skill, access, and commitment. Strictly speaking, national military power exists only in relation to particular other nations and regarding particular conflict situations. This is *actual* military power. However, nations may also have *latent* or *potential* military power in the sense that political leaders and military staffs speculate about hypothetical power relationships—that is to say, they are aware of likely power relationships that would obtain if particular countries were pitted against each other under particular circumstances. In that sense, we may speak more generally about the utility of military power and, in the following, I usually refer to this wider meaning when I use the term.

States also have reputations for military power. They enjoy power prestige, or power images which rest on the perceptions and expectations of other governments and which, though related to actual and potential power, are not necessarily faithful reflections of actual power. Also, like power within other political systems,[5] power in the international system has varying scope—that is to say, it may be greater and more usable for some purposes than for others.

There are many international transactions that are wholly or largely unaffected by differences in power. In the solution of various problems, cooperation or other forms of coordinated interaction create benefits for all participants. These are not benefits secured by one state at the expense of another, but benefits produced by the very act of cooperation, in which all participating countries will share. Even then, to be sure, power may be exerted in order to determine the size of the shares; but many forms of international cooperation—such as on maritime safety measures, means of international communication, and matters of commerce—do not attract the intrusion of power.

However, as happens in any political system, the actors in the international system are apt to frustrate one another in the pursuit of many of their interests; and influence, including military power, may be exerted in order to resolve these conflicts of interest. It is the resolution of conflicts, the allocation of scarce values among states, that international politics is all about.

There are three main determinants of national military power. One is military power *potential*—that is, resources capable of being mobilized for the establishment of military forces. The second determinant is the *value* placed on military power by a nation, and hence the proportion of potential actually transformed into military strength. The third is the *skill* with which re-

[5] *Ibid.*, p. 53.

sources are cast into ready military strength and with which the use of the resulting military power is directed politically as well as militarily. As nations vary markedly in all three conditions, so the distribution of military power in the international system is highly uneven. Up to a point, differences in any one of these conditions may be offset, at any one time, by compensating differences in the others; and over time, the distribution of military power is modified as these basic conditions undergo change.

Statesmen use war or the threat of war as an instrument of statecraft because they expect political utility from its employment. It is *political* utility precisely because resort to force is an allocative mechanism, because it is a major, though by no means the only, basis on which the competition of states for various objects of value is settled; it is meant to affect the international distribution of such things as territory, trade, security, diplomatic influence, prestige, and of power itself. The aim of conflict resolution is to accommodate, formally or informally, the national wills and interests in a particular international conflict; and military force is a form of power that sustains will. In the absence of war, diplomacy may be the salient method for settling conflict. But as, to begin with, the choice of foreign policy is determined by a government's perception of the external environment, including power relationships, so power is often introduced into the diplomatic process. Explicitly in the form of threats or implicitly through silent calculation, considerations of military power act as counters in diplomatic bargaining so that, in any serious dispute, diplomacy is a trial of influence and strength, including military strength, even though it is also a test of wits and skill.

THE DIMINISHED VALUE OF TERRITORIAL CONQUEST

We now turn to the question of whether some foreign-policy objectives on behalf of which military power has been employed frequently in the past have diminished in value. There is the strong impression that territorial conquest by force of arms has lost the perennial attraction it possessed throughout mankind's violent history.[6] In the pre-modern, pre-industrial world, territorial conquest often seemed worthwhile, whether it meant the capture of hunting grounds or farmland, or control of mineral deposits, or access to the sea or to manpower (including slaves), or the diminution of an external military threat, or the incorporation of populations related by such ties as race, language, and religion. Thus, until recently, European history involved an unending series of territorial conquests in Europe; and after European nations had begun to industrialize, it was easy for them to conquer vast areas outside Europe whose populations were greatly inferior militarily and usually put up little resistance, so that, by the end of the nineteenth century, Europeans had not only colonized the entire Western hemisphere and Oceania, but also acquired colonial control over most of Africa and Asia. In Europe itself territory changed ownership with striking frequency, usually as a result of war and conquest, whether in the pursuit of empire, dynastic glory, religious hegemony, or economic advantage; and when national self-determination became a strong political force in the

---

[6] This has been observed by several students of international relations—e.g., Raymond Aron, *Paix et guerre entre les nations*, Paris: Calmann-Lévy, 1962, p. 368; F. H. Hinsley, *Power and the Pursuit of Peace*, Cambridge, Eng.: Cambridge University Press, 1963, p. 358; George Modelski, "Agraria and Industria: Two Models of the International System," in Klaus Knorr and Sidney Verba (eds.), *The International System*, Princeton: Princeton University Press, 1961, p. 142.

nineteenth century, war assisted in the formation of national states.

Nor was territorial conquest always acquisitive. Often it was defensive, involving the restoration of a *status quo ante* previously upset by an aggressor; or it was essentially defensive in terms of considerations of the balance of power; or it was defensive in terms of preserving established access to foreign markets, sources of supply, and investment outlets—as, for example, when the acquisition of overseas colonies by European powers was motivated by the fear that other nations would lay claim to these territories and then restrict commercial access to them.

As will be proposed in Chapter III, the appetite for territorial conquest has become jaded in part because, for some nations at least and in many regions of the world, the military, political, and moral costs of conquest have risen sharply above past levels. However, there are also powerful reasons to suspect that the expected value of conquest has fallen decisively. It is our hypothesis that this has happened chiefly because the leadership in economically developed countries has largely discarded traditional concepts of the value of conquered territory and populations. The political and economic leaders of industrial and wealthy countries are now aware that domestic saving and investment and the advancement of education, science, and technology are the most profitable means and the most secure avenues to the attainment of wealth and welfare. The historical record seems to support this enlightened view. Thus, Switzerland and Sweden have grown wealthy without conquest, over several centuries; and the national incomes of West Germany and Japan, countries that were grossly impoverished during World War II, have in two brief postwar decades expanded at a stupendous rate. Military power may be required for the protection of wealthy societies, but the way to national riches is investment in new capital, better education, and technological research and innovation, rather than in armies, navies, and air forces.

The conditions that have caused the value of territorial conquest to be reappraised are far from clear; but they seem intimately connected with the inception and gradual onsweep of the scientific and industrial revolution in the West. Prior to this revolution and its gathering impact, per capita incomes were incapable of rapid growth, if of any growth at all, except by means of successful conquest. Thus, the levels of production and consumption and the civilization of the free citizens of ancient Athens could scarcely have been reached and maintained on any other basis than the exploitation of conquered areas and slaves. Economic advance in pre-industrial Europe, and no doubt outside Europe, was similarly confined. The mercantilist literature of the seventeenth and eighteenth centuries reflects the view of a world in which what one nation gains another must lose, and in which aggression often seemed the most copious source of profit. Though declining in acceptance, mercantilist and quasi-mercantilist thinking persisted through the nineteenth and the first part of the twentieth century. To the discerning mind, the true sources of wealth have been apparent for some time. But economics, the science concerned with the understanding of wealth, required a long time to mature and develop its present sophistication. It inevitably took longer for its insights to be absorbed and acted upon by the political elites. Indeed, it was a precondition of this development that rationality, including the application of new and specialized knowledge, slowly asserted its claim to put traditional wisdom in matters of statecraft to the tests of truth and relevance.

It also seems that world economic development and technological progress have rendered highly developed countries less dependent on foreign sources of supply than was still true half a century ago or less. At first, economic development and industrialization made the leading European countries less self-sufficient economically as international specialization followed comparative production advantages, a consequence that was noted with some alarm to have serious drawbacks in time of war, when trade routes might be cut off by enemy action. Yet this consequence has lost importance as the nature of war has changed, and the trend itself has evidently become weakened, if not reversed. Nevertheless, there remain exceptions to this change. The European nations, for instance, are now extremely dependent on imports of oil from overseas. It is also clear that the sudden cessation of all imports of vital raw materials and foodstuffs would be highly disturbing to the industrial nations. But this risk is exceedingly remote. It is hard to imagine a combination of circumstances—prolonged war engulfing most of the globe, and adverse concerted action by numerous governments—that might produce such a result. The overseas countries of European settlement are the only large exporters of food, and of many industrial raw materials as well. World economic development has opened up and keeps opening up new sources of supply; even if Western Europe's access to oil from the Near East were completely interrupted, supplies from the Americas could, in an emergency, meet Europe's basic needs. Moreover, technological progress has greatly increased the range of available materials and the ability of modern industries to substitute one material for another without undue loss in efficiency and costs. Over the past two decades, technological progress in agriculture has enormously enhanced food production precisely in the industrial and developed countries—not only in the United States, Canada, and the Antipodes, but also in Western Europe—an area that has become far less dependent on food imports than it was before World Wars I and II. The traditional fear of being cut off from vital foreign sources of supply in time of war has lessened significantly, in part because the changed nature of war has depreciated the kind of economic war potential that was important before the nuclear age, and in part because, even without the emergence of nuclear arms, modern technology was causing raw materials to decline in importance as a component of economic war potential.[7] As far as the manufacture of military equipment is concerned, the importance of raw materials has greatly declined in comparison with scientific, technological, and managerial inputs—that is to say, human resources of a high order.

Recent developments also suggest that the wealthy industrial countries have become less dependent for their economic well-being and growth on foreign markets and foreign investment opportunities than their leaders thought was the case until a few decades ago. Of course, their exports have expanded. They have assisted in bringing about increasing prosperity, and they are essential in earning foreign exchange for the import of vital supplies. Yet modern economic knowledge also shows that nations can make their domestic

[7] Cf. Klaus Knorr, *The War Potential of Nations*, Princeton: Princeton University Press, 1956, chaps. 3, 10; Mancur Olson, Jr., "American Materials Policy and the 'Physiocratic Fallacy,'" *Orbis*, vi (Winter 1963), pp. 670-88.

markets more capacious in order to absorb a rising volume of products. Similarly, it is now perceived that there are essentially unending opportunities for domestic investment.* A world that has understood Keynes and post-Keynesian economics has no need to conquer territory for the sake of national economic gain.

None of this is to deny that international economic specialization and trade are productive of vast benefits to participating nations, or that many individual enterprises may not find it more profitable to sell, buy, or invest abroad than at home. But the important facts are that the foreign trade of the wealthy countries has not in recent decades expanded as much as their annual incomes—much to the distress and chagrin of the less developed countries that are highly dependent on exporting primary products; that—in terms of their foreign commerce—the highly developed countries are each other's best customers, and the less developed and militarily weak countries of lesser importance;† and, above

* In 1965, *cumulative* private investments abroad by the United States were estimated at about $15 billion. This is a small sum if compared with an *annual* U.S. rate of gross new investments amounting to about $100 billion in 1963-65. It is also interesting to note that U.S. direct private investments abroad have been growing much more rapidly in other developed countries than in the underdeveloped world. Investments in the latter accounted for around one-half in 1950, but for only one-third by 1965.

† Thus, between 1949-50 and 1961-62, the average annual exports of 12 highly developed countries (United States, United Kingdom, Austria, Denmark, France, West Germany, Italy, Japan, the Netherlands, Norway, Switzerland, Canada) to a similar set of 14 developed countries (United States, Canada, United Kingdom, Belgium-Luxembourg, France, West Germany, the Netherlands, Austria, Denmark, Iceland, Ireland, Norway, Sweden, Switzerland) expanded by 182 per cent, whereas their exports to Latin America, Middle East, Africa, and all of Asia (excluding the USSR) grew by only 88 per cent. Without the extension of economic aid by the rich to the poorer countries, the figure for exports would have been lower—that is, a sizable proportion of these exports were unrequited.

all, that the understanding of the sources of national wealth has undergone a drastic revision. As a result, the appeal of territorial conquest on economic grounds has greatly decreased. It seems as if, at an advanced stage of industrial and concomitant developments, there were an inverse relationship between the level of economic progress and propensity to territorial conquest.

Two additional factors may be suggested as having contributed to the recent diminution of territorial conquest as a valuable objective of states. First, the forcible acquisition of foreign territory and populations is of lesser value on military grounds, partly because of the declining importance of economic war potential, partly because mere manpower is a minor, if not a dubious, asset in the sort of wars that might occur in the future, and partly because modern technology, notably including military technology, has reduced, though not eliminated for some kinds of war, the importance of foreign bases. Second, except for the division of Germany— admittedly a major exception—and a few minor trouble spots (such as the Italian Tirol), the Western European nations, which have precipitated so many wars in the past, are no longer at loggerheads over problems of national self-determination, and irredentism has therefore virtually disappeared.

Throughout this essay, there will be occasion to emphasize the conditionality of the problem under discussion, and hence the very narrow limits placed on sensible generalization. The deflated appeal of territorial conquest is a telling case in point. This appeal has

(Data compiled from United Nations, *Direction of Trade*, annual, 1958-62; International Monetary Fund, *International Financial Statistics*, 1963-64 Supplement; W. S. and E. S. Woytinsky, *World Commerce and Governments, Trends and Outlook*, New York: Twentieth Century Fund, 1955.)

shrunk probably much more, and certainly more distinctly, in the relatively wealthy industrial nations—in Europe, including Eastern Europe and the USSR, in North America, in Australasia, and in Japan—than among the many new and less developed countries of the world. It is possible that the desire for economic gain, or for relief from economic misery and distress, will direct the eyes of leaders in these less fortunate countries to the conquest of farmlands and other economic assets abroad. Not only are modern concepts of the sources of national wealth more familiar to leaders in the industrial nations than to those in the underdeveloped world, but the rich nations also command the means—the potent and almost painless capacity to save, educate, invent, and innovate—that the poorer peoples usually lack and find so hard to develop.

More important than this international difference in the economic attraction of conquest may be the appeal to incorporate territories and populations in Asia and Africa where present political boundaries—often drawn arbitrarily by former imperialist powers—pay scant attention to ethnic groupings and historical connections. Numerous examples come readily to mind: the division of Korea and Vietnam; unsettled frontier disputes between Communist China, on the one hand, and India and the Soviet Union, on the other; the separation of Taiwan from mainland China; foreign-ruled enclaves such as Hong Kong and Macao; the frontier quarrel between Thailand and Cambodia over the Angkor region; disputes between India and Pakistan over Kashmir, the Rann of Cutch, and other frontier districts; present or potential troubles between the Philippines and Indonesia, Pakistan and Afghanistan, Algeria and Morocco, Ethiopia and Somaliland. Moreover, many of the less developed countries—such as Malaysia, Burma, Thailand, and the Congo—incorporate unassimilated ethnic groups that may aspire to independence and resort to violence in order to achieve it. This holds true also of the Republic of South Africa and of the remnants of former colonial empires. Surely, on account of these factors, the political map of Western Europe and the Americas looks far more settled than that of Africa and Asia. Even within what Soviet leaders used to call the "socialist camp," local nationalisms seem to be recrudescent and present political boundaries may be challenged before long.

There is one additional factor, highly speculative and only indirectly or obscurely connected with the motives thus far examined, that may—once again, in the rich industrial nations—account, beyond a disinterest in territorial conquest, more generally for a recent and perhaps basic decline in foreign-policy goals that made for the offensive, acquisitive use of military power in the past. Some observers have noted a trend in the rich countries concerned toward decreasing political preoccupation with external affairs, or at least a basic preference for grappling with domestic problems, a turning inward on themselves, and a view of the international environment as a primarily distracting burden.[8]

Neither the strength nor the extent of this tendency is known to me, nor do I firmly understand the conditions that brought it about. I do, however, believe in its presence and see its origin mainly in the fact that, in the industrial societies, populations tend to be politically highly mobilized, closely integrated in the political system, and the leaders more responsive to mass preferences than was the case in traditional societies. If committed to politics, the bulk of populations, as many polls

[8] Cf. Charles A. McClelland, "The Acute International Crisis," in Knorr and Verba (eds.), *The International System*, p. 198.

and studies have shown, are interested in the politics of what affects and surrounds them immediately. They are much more concerned with local and especially national than with international affairs; and their governments tend to be heavily committed to the business of the "welfare state." Widespread interest in foreign affairs is sporadic. These populations may respond, and be made to react strongly, and on occasion even excessively, to an aggressive challenge from the outside world, and then approve of, if not demand, the defensive use of military power. Usually, however, they are disinclined to push their governments toward foreign-policy goals requiring a militarily aggressive stance. They seem to sense that any concentration of interest on foreign affairs will absorb energies and other resources otherwise available for coping with domestic problems and promoting domestic welfare.

No doubt, other and related developments have contributed to this tendency to accord a relatively high priority to domestic affairs. Thus, foreign adventures in the past tended to benefit certain influential individuals and groups to the detriment of others; and as industrial societies turned more democratic in political structure and process, support for such ventures was less easily stimulated and decreased notably.

This turning inward in the highly industrialized societies should not lead to exaggerated expectations. We are speaking of a trend, and the forces behind no one trend are strong enough to rule out divergent behavior. Given our frail capacity to conjecture about future events, we must also concede that contrary forces may arise, swell, and overwhelm propensities observable at present. Even if the forces behind the trend are strong and persist, we must not forget that "history," when it moves "forward," is apt to move "like a crab skirting a boulder."[9] Although most European imperial powers dissolved their colonial empires after World War II, they did so under pressure and with obvious reluctance in several cases, and in some instances only after a considerable struggle. One cannot be sure that these were the last reflexes of an old and dying impulse. As is normal in any process of change, the break with past political institutions, ideas, and practices is never clean, and some interest groups will continue, or try to continue, to maintain and use such relics to their advantage. The activities of the Katanga lobby in Britain's attempt to salvage business assets after the Belgian Congo became independent are an example. Moreover, we do not know whether this turning inward will also manifest itself in the large Communist nations as they become more developed economically and wax affluent; nor, finally, does the trend observed in mature industrial, urbanized, and democratic nations preclude the arousal of mass support for military ventures abroad, although for purposes that, by our definition, are defensive rather than acquisitive. This has surely happened in the United States, which has imposed on itself the burden of containing what its government perceives as aggressive expansionist moves under Communist direction. This country may at times serve this mission with excessive zeal, with a crude conception of the political forces with which it must deal, and with an overemphasis on the use of military means. Its reactions to Communist threats in the Caribbean and the rest of the Western hemisphere tend to be explosive and subject to strong emotional outbursts. Yet no one familiar with the United States, and unbiased in judgment, will deny that this country plays its role with a palpable and basic reluctance. It is

[9] Geoffrey Barraclough, *History in a Changing World*, Norman: University of Oklahoma Press, n.d., p. 204.

not fighting in South Vietnam, as it did not fight in Korea, with anything resembling enthusiasm; and in the articulation of American foreign policy, and the demeanor of recent American Presidents, one detects none of the symbols reminiscent of the country's brief flirtation, around the turn of the century, with an imperialist "manifest destiny."*

* If one believes it to be true that the affluent societies of the West exhibit a defensive behavior and prefer investing their energies in promoting domestic welfare; if, in other words, this change in relevant attitudes is deemed to express not merely a temporary swing, then one is compelled to reject not only the Marxist-Leninist theory of mature capitalism but also more recent theories, propounded in the United States, that see this country as transferring itself into a "warfare state"—theories that seemed to receive appreciable support from President Eisenhower's vague warning about a "military-industrial complex" engaged in pressing for a high or excessive level of defense expenditures.

There is indeed little evidence that the United States has become a "warfare state" whose government and policies are dominated by a coalition of the military and business interests heavily involved in defense production. The relatively most respectable propounder of the thesis was C. Wright Mills, especially in his major work on *The Power Elite* (New York: Oxford University Press, 1956). According to his view, the United States was being ruled increasingly by a single unified "power elite" composed of business, military "warlords," and a political elite which, infiltrated and subverted by the stronger business elite, was by far the weakest of the three groups. Mills's work was basically defective. He used fragmentary evidence and a distorting conceptual apparatus in order to produce a highly biased view of American society. Thus, he failed to appreciate the dynamics of a maturing industrial society and ignored the fact that the drastic changes in United States foreign and military policy reflected the altered position of the United States in a world which was deeply unsettled and in which the weakening of several of the great powers of the past and the process of de-colonization tended to engender, in many regions, a power vacuum into which the Soviet Union was apparently prepared to move on behalf of its revolutionary objectives. The defects of the Mills thesis have been lucidly demonstrated by Talcott Parsons in "The Distribution of Power in American Society," *World Politics*, x (October 1957), pp. 123-43.

Other writers, non-academic and in the radical muckraking tradi-

As already conceded, it is again the wealthy industrial nations in which this turning inward is mainly observed or postulated. But it does seem to extend to developing countries of lesser wealth, such as Mexico, Chile, and Burma. On the other hand, one is struck by the phenomenon of the Sukarnos, Nassers, Ben Bellas, and Nkrumahs, who seem to devote an inordinate proportion of their energies to foreign affairs. To be sure, their emphasis on foreign politics and policies is not necessarily farfetched or gratuitous. In part, for reasons already advanced in this chapter, their national and international problems differ grossly from those faced by the leadership of the highly developed nations. In addition, they feel strongly about the remnants of old-fashioned imperialism and are fearful of new forms of imperialism succeeding the old; and even if they are preoccupied with solving the domestic problems of their countries, and particularly with promoting economic growth, they are attracted to all possibilities of securing the largest possible assistance from the wealthiest nations. The only point to be made here is that there can be no question in these cases, and in the underdeveloped world as a whole, of turning inward and of a relevant disinterest in foreign affairs and hence of lessened occasions, on this ground, for the use of military power.

These, then, are the changes notable to this observer that indicate a recently diminished interest in foreign-policy goals which traditionally inspired an abundant

---

tion, have produced popularized and vulgarized versions of the Mills theory, usually adding to it a conspiratorial theory which Mills himself had eschewed. An example is Fred J. Cook, *The Warfare State*, New York: Macmillan, 1963. For my review of Cook's work, see "Warfare and Peacefare States and the Costs of Transition: A Review," *Journal of Conflict Resolution*, vii (July 1963), pp. 754-57.

use of military power. First, there seems to be in important parts of the world a distinctly smaller interest in territorial conquest for economic and military advantage, and for consolidating populations on the basis of national self-determination—a development, however, that does not necessarily preclude the desire for territorial conquest on other grounds. Second, the industrial and wealthy states, oriented toward the achievement of mass welfare, tend to be preoccupied with the pursuit of domestic tasks and to take an essentially defensive interest in foreign-policy matters. That these developments are more conspicuous in, or largely confined to, the economically highly developed countries does not deprive them of importance, for these nations are also, by and large, the militarily powerful. This is indicated by the fact that, together, and including the USSR, they account for over 80 per cent of the world's military expenditures.[10]

THE REMAINING USES OF MILITARY POWER

We are unable to infer, however, that these developments, remarkable as they are, have diminished the political utility of national military power. No such overall appraisal is feasible. The fact is that there remain plenty of other goals whose achievement is conditional on relations of military strength. Thus, the leaders of nation-states evidently remain convinced that their independence—that is to say, their ability to function as autonomous structures—is made more secure by military forces and alliances. Moreover, the militant competition of ideologies may render international understanding and peace more precarious than they were

[10] Cf. United Nations, Dept. of Economic and Social Affairs, *Economic and Social Consequences of Disarmament*, New York, 1962, pp. 4, 62.

a century ago,[11] and ideologically inspired militancy may stimulate, not perhaps an appetite for territorial conquest, but the desire that territories change political systems and leaders, if necessary and feasible by force. Indeed, while the world has become more integrated, so that it constitutes a continuous field of political and military actions, it is a field charged with deep political and ideological divisions and antagonisms. In many poor countries there is suspicion and envy of the rich societies. In many ex-colonial areas there is an undertow of resentment and hostility toward the ex-imperialist powers which in some instances involves animosities based on differences in race and color. The elites in many of the new and underdeveloped countries have a strong appetite for asserting themselves in world politics, a remarkable *Geltungsdrang*,[12] despite the weak military and economic base from which they operate. Above all, there are at present two issues that mark deep cleavages in international relations. One is the genuine fear of neo-imperialism or neo-colonialism in the underdeveloped world. Thus, Ben Bella, until June 1965 President of Algeria, announced that "real independence" required "economic liberation" as well as political independence, that "colonialism" and "imperialism" have appeared in new forms "to perpetuate their domination," to preserve "through channels of economic and even cultural relations, certain ties by means of which they prevent the development of countries which were under its direct influence."[13] This attitude is assiduously promoted by Communist spokesmen. Thus, the

[11] Aron, *Paix et guerre*, p. 767.

[12] Cf. R. Soerjono Wirjodiatmodjo, *Der Gedanke der Blockfreiheit in Südostasien*, Stuttgart: Kohlhammer, 1964, p. 118.

[13] *Global Digest* (Hong Kong), II (May 1965), pp. 160f. The statements were made at the opening session of the Afro-Asian Economic Seminar in February 1965.

"new colonialism" aims to "implant capitalism in Africa, Asia and Latin America, to gain control over the socio-economic development of these countries. . . ."[14] And the other issue is presented by the Communists, who are still saying that they look forward to a world from which what they call capitalist—and eventually, indeed, all non-Communist—governments have vanished. These two issues governing the "East-West" struggle, and giving rise to a so-called "North-South" tension, create deep, ramified, and to some extent overlapping cleavages. In addition to numerous local issues, they provide plenty of the stuff of conflict from which violence may erupt.

Thus, the present international system is rife with interconnected tensions, conflicts, and instabilities. It is inhabited by numerous political communities whose elites regard the military power, political activities, and ideological commitments of other states as a threat to their own independence, political order, and basic values. In such a world, it is natural that statesmen wish to control their environment as much as possible and, allied with other states pursuing congruent interests, seek to make this environment as conducive as possible to the satisfaction of their common interests, and perhaps even covet conquest for this reason. What all states desire is a "compatible" world and hence they want to limit, if not overcome, the power of hostile states and groupings by interposing their countervailing power if they can do so. Though there are important forms of power other than the military, national military force is one form they dare not neglect and from which they expect to derive political utility of a high order. This utility we are unable to measure, because it is essentially subjective. Thus, even though territorial conquest has

[14] Y. Oganisyan, "New Frontiers of Old Colonialism," *International Affairs* (Moscow), June 1965, p. 33.

lost importance as an external objective of states, there may have occurred only a shift in, rather than a diminution of, the objectives for the pursuit of which military power is valued by national governments. Indeed, it is possible that for some states the value of military power for defensive use has risen in recent decades. This may have happened because what they perceive to need defense from external aggression is not some particular economic or political advantage, but a whole way of life—that is to say, the very integrity of society. Furthermore, since some aggression is now of a worldwide scope, foreign policy and the use of military force must be commensurate with this global scale. Surely, at this time the United States entertains absolutely no desire to conquer foreign territories. Nevertheless, this country is maintaining military forces in being that are larger, however measured, than they have ever been when we were not engaged in large-scale war. As we suggested, this power is directed to serve essentially defensive purposes, including the preservation of a world order in which the United States, and other societies of the same political and economic character, are able to prosper.

We are thus led to conclude that, if the political utility of national military power has suffered an appreciable and—as some observers maintain—a dramatic decline, this has probably not happened, or not happened mainly, because the uses of military power have become irrelevant or less relevant to the valued objectives that statesmen seek to pursue. The decline in utility must have been caused chiefly, if not wholly, by an increase in the disadvantages or costs attached to the use of military power on behalf of foreign-policy objectives. In the following chapters we shall turn to an analysis of these costs.

CHAPTER III

SOME RESTRAINTS ON THE

USE OF MILITARY POWER

THE WIDESPREAD IMPRESSION that the costs of using national military power have risen strikingly, and that the political utility of employing military force has suffered a corresponding decline, reflects primarily the emergence and unprecedented destructiveness of nuclear weapons and their associated delivery vehicles. To this problem we will turn in Chapter IV. The present chapter is devoted to other conditions that have caused the costs of applying military forces for some purposes to mount, and have thus generated a set of palpable restraints. Some of these restraints are not as new as those produced by nuclear weaponry. The latter appeared just as suddenly as the weapons themselves, and as their nature was appreciated. Some of the restraints discussed in this chapter can be traced back into the more remote past. These are new only in the sense that they represent a marked increment over whatever restraints warfare was subject to traditionally. Their growth has gathered momentum since World War I and, together with other restraints of more recent origin, has made the resort to military power for some purposes more costly than was the case until half a century ago.

THE RESTRICTED LEGITIMACY OF WAR

The attitudes of European societies toward military power and war were strangely contradictory between the time of the French Revolution and World Wars I and II. They were attitudes as incompatible as the two faces of a Janus head: one side favored war, the other favored its restriction and control. No doubt, these contradictions resulted from the rapid transition of these societies from a past still dominated by feudal and aristocratic institutions and values to the wealthy, industrial, and basically democratic mass society of the present era.

We may sketch the features of the face favoring war by beginning with the genesis of mass nationalism and militarism in the age of the French Revolution and the Napoleonic empire. European nationalism served industrializing societies as a new force of social cohesion when traditional, pre-industrial bonds and loyalties gradually lost their hold and finally crumbled away. Pre-industrial ruling groups, at first still exercising a great deal of power, identified themselves with and manipulated this new political force to their advantage. They were in a position to do so because the extension of the suffrage to new classes of citizens was gradual, and because the newcomers were insufficiently enfranchised in terms of comprehending the new forces at work in the industrializing societies. This rendered them still more or less subject to the hold of traditional appeals and hence to political seduction by traditional ruling groups that, seen from a longer perspective, were definitely on the decline. In several key countries—and most notably in Germany and Austria-Hungary—these groups continued to control diplomacy and the military establishment. As a revolutionary spirit developed in the growing ranks of industrial labor and in part of what the Marxists came to call the "intelligentsia," the older ruling groups—joined and in some countries gradually replaced by leading elements of the ascending middle classes—exploited the nationalist idea for anti-revolutionary purposes. Militarism was one upshot of this development. Although its beginnings can be traced to the early Romantic Age, it became a formidable force only in the second half of the nineteenth century, standing for "a dominion of military man over the civilian, an undue preponderance of military demands, an emphasis on military considerations, spirit, ideals, and scales of value, in the life of states."[15]

European militarism found various expressions and served many purposes. It supported the claims of the church, the nobility, and the officer class. As exemplified in the writings of Thiers and Maurras in France, Treitschke in Germany, and Carlyle and Kipling in England, the representatives of militarism inspired a cult of force, extolled the traditional virtues of the warrior, romanticized war, and applied the theories of Darwin to human society, describing the life of nations as a perpetual struggle for power through which only the fittest survived. As symbolized by the Dreyfus affair in France, the supporters of militarism maligned, and conspired against, those who refused to give the armed nation-state its full due; and they began to favor new concepts of racial superiority, as in the writings of Count Gobineau and H. S. Chamberlain. Militarism found expression in the introduction of universal military service in time of peace, first in Prussia and then—after her decisive victories over Austria-Hungary in 1866, and over France in 1870-1871—in France and other continental nations. Militarism induced a new imperialist scramble, leading to the establishment of vast overseas colonies in Africa and Asia—areas regarded as

[15] Alfred Vagts, *A History of Militarism*, New York: Norton, 1937, p. 12. See also *ibid.*, pp. 15-20; Emil Obermann, *Soldaten, Bürger, Militaristen*, Stuttgart: Cotta, 1958, pp. 219ff.; Hinsley, *Power and the Pursuit of Peace*, pp. 119ff.

terra nullius, according to European concepts of international law, that might be acquired by simple "discovery" and "occupation." The militarist dispensation provided urban populations with the spectacle of glamorous parades and other military pageantry. Even where democratic forms of government were gradually adopted and strengthened, the militarist philosophy prevented the evolution of doctrines and institutions permitting effective civilian control over the military.[16] Only the successful hold of militarism on the masses of European peoples can explain the broad popularity of war in 1914, the beginning of a struggle that "was fought on a basis that was bound to give maximum scope to hysteria and frenzies associated with the fury of battles,"[17] and that displayed, as one historian called it, a "somnambulant heroism."[18] And finally, militarism culminated in the savage mass movements of Fascism in Italy and Nazism in Germany.

These are, in brief, the features of the face that affirmed the need for national military power, legitimized war, and showed no eagerness to tolerate limits on the use of military force. This is the face that was turned to the past, when war was still the sport of lords and kings and when, traditionally, the employment of force was permitted for any reason. Yet there is also the other face, only dimly featured at the beginning of the period and much more clearly defined at its end. It is presumably a forward-looking face, expressing a quite different attitude toward international war and the uses of power in international affairs.

[16] Vagts, *A History of Militarism,* pp. 166-75.

[17] Herbert Butterfield, *Christianity, Diplomacy and War,* London: Epworth Press, 1953, p. 177.

[18] William H. McNeill, *The Rise of the West,* Chicago: University of Chicago Press, 1963, p. 742.

Ideas and dreams of controlling war and perhaps establishing the conditions of permanent peace appeared early in European history. They are manifest in the natural-law tradition of "just war," and over the centuries bolder notions were expressed in the writings of such men as Dante and Dubois, Crucé and Sully, Saint-Pierre and Kant, Bentham and James Mill.[19] But there is a big difference between an idea propounded by a few individuals and small groups and one that gathers a substantial following and acquires political weight. Like militarism and nationalism, the beginnings of such a force in Europe can be dated back to the early nineteenth century. The exhausting wars of the French Revolution and the Napoleonic era touched off a brief period of idealistic pacifism; and around the middle of the century, influential sections of the rising class of entrepreneurs embraced a liberal creed in politics as well as in economics. Schumpeter may be right in insisting that trade is an utterly different method from conquest for procuring goods and services, and that only the transitory survival of feudal values and structures prevented the liberal-capitalist ideology—as represented by the Cobdenites and the Manchester School—from prevailing over the outmoded attitudes of the past.[20] In the last third of the century, the bulk of the new middle class turned conservative in most European countries, and it was the nationalist and militarist forces that were in the saddle. Nevertheless, anti-militarism became an increasingly significant political force as the socialist parties succeeded in organizing a substantial proportion of the expanding industrial labor force. The large socialist parties in France and Germany proclaimed the international solidarity of the proletariat,

[19] Hinsley, *Power and the Pursuit of Peace*, Part I.
[20] Schumpeter, *Imperialism and Social Classes*, chap. 5.

advocated the abolition of professional armies and the adoption of citizen militias, and roundly condemned wars of aggression.[21] As the century drew to a close, some voices—such as that of the Polish banker Ivan Bloch—warned of the drift toward war and the shape it might take, and the initiative of Tsar Nicholas II led to the two peace conferences at The Hague. Measured against the debacle that was to come, these conferences achieved little. Indeed, when the conference of 1899 opened, "speculation was rife as to whether or not it could last a fortnight without ending in a quarrel, and perhaps precipitating a general war";[22] and Yan Yu, a Chinese observer at the first Hague Conference, leaving a committee room one day, sadly shook his head and remarked: "Too much talkee-talkee, too little doee-doee."[23] When the big war erupted, the second International of the socialists proved ineffective; the French and German workers quickly succumbed to the appeal of patriotism.

The protracted carnage of World War I made a difference. It produced a revulsion from militarism and war that found expression, on the one hand, in the isolationist posture of the United States and, on the other, in the war-guilt clause of the Treaty of Versailles, in the establishment of the League of Nations, in several disarmament conferences, and in the Kellogg Pact of 1928 which, for the first time, established the outlawry of all aggressive war as an international convention. After World War I, there was a sturdy anti-war spirit not only in Great Britain, France, and the United States—nations

---

[21] Cf. Milorad M. Crachkovitch, *Les socialismes français et allemands et le problème de la guerre, 1870-1914*, Geneva: Droz, 1953.

[22] Frederick W. Holls, *The Peace Conference at The Hague*, New York: Macmillan, 1900, Preface, viii.

[23] *Ibid.*, p. 326.

aghast at the costs and disillusioned with the fruits of victory—but also, during the 1920's, in Germany. When Germany threatened war again in the 1930's, she and Italy were propelled by radical political movements that displayed ample signs of atavistic reaction and that were, in large part at least, perhaps a last revolt and ugly perversion of social forces and ideals that belonged to the pre-industrial world and were on the wane. Britain, France, and the United States, on the other hand, were extremely reluctant to intervene by force before the Axis threat was backed by a formidable military organization. In fact, it was their profound weariness of war which Hitler tried to exploit to his advantage in the hope that great victories could be achieved without large-scale war.[24]

There were not in 1939, as there had been in 1914, enthusiastic crowds thronging the streets of capital cities when hostilities had broken out. Appeals to national military glory were notably absent. Even in Nazi Germany, the majority of the population was apprehensive and glum. The massacres of World War II reinforced the revulsion from war experienced toward the end of and after World War I; and the Nuremberg trials, the establishment of the United Nations, and various disarmament conferences have reflected widespread and persistent hopes that war, as an instrument of statecraft, can be brought under firm control. Anxieties and hopes have no doubt been further fanned by awareness of the immense destructiveness of nuclear armaments. But they had acquired a strong basis longer in the making. Although these developments originated largely in the West, their importance was world-wide, for it was after all an oligarchy of Western great powers,

[24] Michael Howard, "Military Power and International Order," *International Affairs* (London), LX (July 1964), p. 402.

excepting Japan, that controlled the world. Moreover, the militarily feeble and the colonial populations outside the West had their own ample reasons for fearing and repudiating the unlimited sway of military might, and their leaders were by no means unsusceptible to Western notions of curbing aggressive military behavior.

What these developments amount to is not only that governments are inclined to approach the international use of military force with considerable wariness, with prudential considerations that act as a substantial restraint in themselves, but that the legitimacy of resorting to uncontrolled violence has been suffering a marked degree of erosion. By "legitimacy" we mean that an act is legitimate when it is accepted from a belief that it is morally right and proper. Up to World War I, the precipitation of war for practically any purpose was regarded as a legitimate act and this was recognized in international law. If the use of international violence is less legitimate today, this results from a widespread change in moral standards,[25] though the geographic distribution of this change is very uneven. As aggressive war has now been outlawed by the United Nations charter, the permissible range of resort to military force has been limited by a concept of "just war,"[26] or at least "permissible war"; and this represents possibly an epochal shift. What may be under way is the inception of new norms and institutions that are to govern the use of violence in interstate relations. If these norms and institutions muster increasing strength and authority, they will do so on the basis of a common world-wide aspiration among nations to cope with a danger of destruction they all more or less share—that is, a common learning

[25] Hinsley, *Power and the Pursuit of Peace*, p. 276.
[26] William D. Coplin, "International Law and Assumptions About the State System," *World Politics*, xvii (July 1965), p. 629.

process stimulated by the recognition that the interests of all are better served by new restraints and controls on the use of military power than by unrestricted resort to the arbitrament of war.

If anything of this significance is actually in the making, the change involved must obviously be propelled by very strong underlying forces. We have sketched, within the Western world, the history of signs that may well be an index of their existence. And it is not perhaps surprising that the erosion of the legitimacy of international warfare made rapid progress after the experience of World Wars I and II. In these wars, civilian suffering and anguish began to be added appreciably to the slaughter at the battle fronts. European war—whose conduct had been limited in objectives, modes of fighting, and consequences for about two centuries, and had been relatively careful of civilian life and property, and hence tolerable as a method of statecraft—turned into "total war." It did so partly for technological reasons, but in part it was also the very shock of its fierce destructiveness that turned World Wars I and II into furious wars "for righteousness" and for the total surrender of the "wicked" and "evil" opponent.[27] It would be astonishing if this new dimension of destruction were not registered by the nations that experienced it.

At this point, we must refer to a hypothesis which may explain why the present revulsion from unrestricted war rests on a fairly effective political foundation. The hypothesis—already suggested by Auguste Comte and Herbert Spencer[28]—is that industrial or, as we say now, modern societies are bereft of some of the dispositions and interests that had made war congenial to more traditional societies, that the ethos of the mature indus-

[27] Butterfield, *Christianity, Diplomacy and War*, pp. 22f.
[28] Cf. Modelski, "Agraria and Industria," *op.cit.*, pp. 118f.

trial society tends to be incompatible with at least some of the traditional preference for war, and for what could be achieved by means of international violence.

For one thing, in traditional societies, the bulk of the population—that is to say, especially the peasants—bore many of the costs of warfare in terms of casualties and of ravaged fields and plundered stock. *The Peloponnesian War* by Thucydides, Caesar's *War Commentaries*, the chronicles of the Thirty Years' War in Europe, and many similar documents vividly portray the plight of these people in countryside and towns. The chroniclers record these happenings simply as matters of fact, without expressions of revulsion or sympathy; and the victimized populations themselves may have felt no grievances because they accepted these costs as the natural order of things, and, if they did feel such costs as grievances, they had usually no way, or only inadequate ways, of influencing their overlords. As societies became industrialized and wealthy, and literacy and education spread, traditional hardships were no longer taken as the foreordained order of things, and governments tended to become more responsive to public sentiment and demands, more responsible for public welfare. Even the liberal concepts of the mid-nineteenth-century middle class now seem strangely outmoded. Its aspirations bear little resemblance to more modern concepts of national and personal welfare. Orthodox liberalism was concerned with removing feudal and other traditional obstacles to rapid economic progress, and with extracting a large volume of savings for investment at a time when affluence was still reserved for a tiny minority of the population. By now these notions have largely given way to concepts aiming at a new rational organization of economic and social life. In fact, in economically advanced societies, the welfare state seems to have become a major political ideal; and it tends to become a reality with little regard to form of government, although its development is perhaps more pronounced where Western procedures of democracy are adopted and governments must renew their mandate periodically in genuinely competitive elections based on universal suffrage. In other words, the bulk of the adult population tends to be politically mobilized in the modern, industrial, and affluent state. This, thus far, has been historical experience; and the historical record also indicates that in such societies militarism tends to decline, the military calling tends to lose its glamor, the emphasis tends to be on private and public expenditures for immediate personal and family welfare—indeed, on ego indulgence—and, as already suggested in Chapter II, the attention of governments tends to turn inward and grow disinclined toward foreign adventures requiring the aggressive, acquisitive use of military power.

Industrialization is, of course, a development that has proceeded for centuries in the Western world. By comparison with the past, the European nations were already industrialized in the nineteenth century, and Germany certainly was in the 1930's; yet these societies certainly did not then show signs of the inward-turning tendency of the modern welfare state. But these were still times which, for the societies involved, marked a relatively early stage of transition. Rapid industrialization came to Germany, Italy, and Japan later than to Britain and France, and German and Italian Fascism can be regarded as a throwback phenomenon, while Japan, in the 1930's, was at a stage of economic development comparable to Germany in the last third of the nineteenth century. The maturation of the industrial welfare state is a very recent phenomenon, certainly of the twentieth century, and probably of the mid-twentieth century.[29]

It might be suggested, finally, that the modern emphasis on the education, health, and welfare of the common man is in fundamental conflict with foreign policies based on regarding man elsewhere as a legitimate object of aggression and oppression. That emphasis rests on a morality that tends to assert the communality of mankind. Moreover, in the affluent industrial welfare state, not only do traditional and pre-industrial values tend to evaporate, but the political power structure lends scant support to the remnants of pre-industrial elites. As government activities expand in scope and increase in complexity, and as the state bureaucracy grows, this bureaucracy tends to be recruited quite differently from that of the European countries in the nineteenth and early twentieth centuries. In the modern welfare state, bureaucracies tend to be professionalized and to recruit their numbers more on the basis of criteria of universal achievement than on the basis of social origin, other particularist criteria, and even political influence. This tends to be true also for the recruitment of military leadership. There is a world of difference between, for example, Britain's officer corps at the time of the Crimean War and at present. In the traditional and early post-traditional societies, military leaders were recruited largely from the nobility and upper class. In the modern society, military leaders, too, tend to be professional specialists; as such they are less wedded to the traditional values of the warrior and aristocrat, and tend to enjoy less social prestige and political power than was characteristic of the officer class of many European nations in the nineteenth century.

[29] Cf. McNeill, *The Rise of the West*, pp. 794ff.

If the dominant attitudes toward war and its legitimacy change as the industrial welfare state comes of age —which is happening only gradually—and becomes oriented toward mass welfare, this shift is obviously momentous. But it is no more so than the observable revision of many other traditional and pre-modern attitudes and practices—for instance, those concerning slavery; the administration of severe punishment for crimes like pilfering and petty larceny, now considered minor; the legitimacy of the death penalty for any crime; or the autocratic structure of family relationships.[30]

As already intimated, we are not saying, of course, that present reality corresponds fully to the model of the wealthy welfare state even in the most developed societies, although the gap is small in countries such as Sweden, Norway, the Netherlands, and Switzerland, where the temptation to indulge in aggressive foreign adventure has been precluded for some time by inferior military potential. Generally speaking, we are in an age of transition, with practices, values, and symbols of the pre-modern past, which die hard, still intermingled with those of the modern state. In nations such as the United States, France, and Great Britain, a sizable, though diminishing, part of the citizenry is still dedicated to the virtues of individual self-reliance (and other quite admirable ancient virtues as well!), and often bitterly opposed to the welfare state. And it is interesting to note that in the United States, for instance, it is the ultra-conservative fringe, a good many of the less extreme conservatives, and usually also the rural communities

[30] Hinsley, *Power and the Pursuit of Peace*, p. 276; Glen H. Elder, Jr., "Role Relations, Sociocultural Environments, and Autocratic Family Ideology," *Sociometry*, xxviii (June 1965), pp. 173-96.

and the less educated public, who tend to be most inclined toward international violence. These conditions simply bespeak the possibility that, as long as the transition to what we have called the modern affluent welfare state is uncompleted, the behavior of industrial states may occasionally revert to the modes of the premodern past. But they also suggest that further urbanization and increased access to education may well strengthen attachment to the newer concepts of social welfare and humane standards.

On the other hand, the erosion in the notion of the broad legitimacy of war is not confined to the developed nations of the West. Beyond its realm, to be sure, popular participation in and support of the relevant attitudes toward war, and their imposition on government, are much more limited. Available evidence seems to indicate that, in this respect, the attitudes of the broad populations in the Soviet Union, Poland, and other Communist countries are little different from those prevailing in the West, but the ability of these populations to make their rulers conform to these attitudes is decidedly less. The limits set to popular participation are, mostly for different reasons, far more severe in the underdeveloped countries and especially in the underdeveloped new states. Typically, the masses of these populations are only beginning to become integrated in state-wide political communities. Most Asian, Latin American, and African peasants are still governed largely by premodern modes of life, and live outside the universe of discourse that is concerned with matters of international order and disorder. But even in the developing countries, the urban elites and the rapidly expanding numbers of educated men are no strangers to this universe. They are "plugged in" on the international system of political communications and share in the complex and troubled attitudes toward war of the present age. Mankind is moving toward a common history and, in some limited respects at least, toward the rudimentary development of a universal human conscience.[31]

We must not forget that, to the extent that a sort of world community is in the making, it is evolving at present under the pressure of impulses, challenges, and ideas originating in the West. It is not only the worldwide transmission of modern technology and science—and the spread of the scientific attitude has itself far-reaching implications for the perspective of the highly educated anywhere—but also the propagation of Western political notions and concepts that governs or affects so much of the world-wide process of modernization. After all, even Communism and modern forms of socialism are Western inventions; and so is modernization itself. If the elites in the developing countries are politically suspicious of, and hostile to, the West, they are so in reaction to the past aggressiveness and, indeed, often the brutality and rapacity of Western nations. But they also are so with minds and thoughts that, in part, have been structured by Western ideas and ideals. Regarding concepts of the legitimacy of war, moreover, the elites in the underdeveloped and new states have the additional stimulus of fear and desperation. Theirs are the militarily weak countries that in a world of unrestricted international violence and military aggression could only suffer defeat at the hands of the highly industrialized states.

The forces tending to restrict resort to international violence achieved a small degree of institutionalization in the United Nations, as they did earlier in the League of Nations, and as they do furthermore in some regional

[31] Aron, *Paix et guerre*, pp. 368f.

organizations. Even though these achievements are decidedly modest, it is a mistake to scoff at the League because it proved impotent in the face of major aggression or, for similar reasons, to belittle the United Nations. These institutions can be regarded as experiments that were bound to court failure and produce disappointment but whose value does not depend upon immediate and full success. They may turn out to be feeble precursors of sturdier attempts at laying down and enforcing some sort of constitution for world politics. Nor can it be said that the United Nations has been wholly ineffective in these matters. It embodies some potential for action on behalf of world peace. After all, it has served to confine some local conflicts and, as demonstrated on the occasion of the fighting between India and Pakistan in 1965, it provides an international forum in which the counsels of restraint can be concentrated, and achieve a cumulative impact. As constituted at the present time, the United Nations cannot, of course, be counted upon to prevent or stop, by collective force, military aggression involving the great powers on opposite sides. In fact, the United Nations was not designed for this purpose.

Whether or not the attitudes behind the narrowed legitimacy of war will grow and lead to the acceptance of still more restrictive norms, and especially to a further institutionalization of controls as yet quite weak, it is, of course, impossible to know. Perhaps these current inhibitions will prove no more significant than the limits imposed on medieval warfare in Europe. Over the long run, beyond doubt, all nations share a strong interest in the avoidance and elimination of international violence, especially violence in a highly destructive form. Over the short run, however, this interest may be less appealing to leaders of some states, and governments everywhere nurse a strong, if not irresistible, penchant to discount the farther future excessively, and to give shorter-run interests priority over the longer-run. Furthermore, intense antagonism over other issues than those of international order may obstruct, and perhaps preclude, agreement on, and the close and continuous cooperation necessary for, the effective minimization of interstate warfare. Finally, there is the dilemma that the noted erosion of the legitimacy of war is associated with the virtual non-erosion of the means of upholding national sovereignty; and that the continued reliance on these national means arises in part from the fact that substitute approaches to security are unavailable.

A specific difficulty is presented by the fact that only one kind of war, not all wars, is now considered illegitimate, and that the distinctions between the legitimate and illegitimate kinds are hard to define in practice. War in defense against aggression, and war for the liberation of oppressed peoples, are exempt from the reduction in the legitimacy of war—the first exception being especially popular in the West, and the second in the Communist and in the ex-colonial countries. The definition of military aggression—a normative and largely subjective concept—has been a notoriously intractable problem. Nobody has ever been able to draw a clear-cut, unmistakable line between military aggression and non-aggression. Precisely for this reason, and also in order to escape or minimize any penalties attached to outright aggression, an aggressor—assuming he is aware of the nature of his behavior—will attempt to obscure the fact of aggression, and shift the responsibility for the origin of the conflict onto the victim. Yet even without deliberate obfuscation, the identity of the aggressor is ambiguous in many actual conflict situations. Two examples from recent United States experience may

illuminate the point. When in 1964 this country fur-
nished aircraft for Belgian paratroopers on a mission to
liberate prisoners of the Congo rebels in Stanleyville,
the United States public thought of this as a humanitar-
ian rescue operation; but many African leaders, as well
as the Communist governments, branded it as an aggressive imperialist action. And when, early in 1965, the
United States began to bomb targets in North Vietnam,
it justified these air raids on the basis that North Vietnam was acting as an aggressor against South Vietnam.
However, since there had been no open military aggression by North Vietnamese forces, it was easy for many
people, and by no means only the Communists, to suspect or conclude that these United States actions constituted aggression. Many of our allies failed to support
the United States in this matter, and even the attentive
public in the United States was divided on the issue.
The British government did support the United States
despite pressure from the left wing of the Labour Party.
But it is interesting to note that, when the United States
government disclosed the use of non-lethal gases in the
South Vietnamese war, Michael Stewart, the British
Foreign Secretary, who was in Washington at the time,
expressed "the very grave concern" felt in Britain about
this use of gas. In an address to the National Press Club,
he continued: "I am, in fact, asking your Government—
to quote your own Declaration of Independence—to display a decent respect for the opinions of mankind."[32]

Aggression may be readily identified when the regular military forces of one state boldly cross the boundary
of another. But even then the issue is not always clear
when traced back to the origins of the conflict; the at-
tacked state may have committed grossly provocative

[32] *New York Times*, March 24, 1965, p. 1.

acts against the other; there is not rarely a plausible regression of "causative" factors; and once an originally defending side gets aroused, it may turn aggressive on its part. But, as we shall have occasion to discuss subsequently, in the present era aggression often proceeds by proxy and other indirection—that is, in much less visible form—and in such cases the compelling identification of an aggressor may often defy human ingenuity. The crucial problem is that, in view of the complexity of real life, no form of words is self-defining. As holds true of much domestic law, its application to a concrete set of circumstances, and the resultant identification of aggression, call for an essentially judgmental act by some body whose authority is generally accepted.[33] But no authoritative decision-maker on matters of war and peace does, at least as yet, exist.

Yet the problem is patently significant, Virtually all governments protest their love of peace, reject aggressions as a means of policy, and ostensibly maintain military forces solely for uses that remain legitimate. The cynic may well incline to the view that nothing significant has really changed, since it is easy for governments to conceal the true situation from the outside world, and to persuade their constituencies, or for people to deceive themselves, that *their* employment of military force conforms to the legitimate cases. Under these circumstances, how effective is the new illegitimacy of the aggressive use of national military power?

Beyond question, its effectiveness is limited and highly conditional. It would be rash, however, to conclude that it is wholly ineffective, a meaningless piety. To begin with, the fact of aggression is often not ob-

[33] Myres S. McDougal and Florentine P. Feliciano, *Law and Minimum World Public Order*, New Haven: Yale University Press, 1961, chaps. 1-4.

scure. Whatever the government of an aggressive nation may think and announce, and whatever its friends and allies may say in its support, the international community of nations is entitled to arrive at a verdict and, in the modern world, it has plenty of means of being informed and of getting the information quickly. In fact, the virtual instantaneousness with which news is today communicated throughout most of the world is a condition quite different from that which obtained until a hundred or so years ago.

Secondly, the new restraint on aggressive war is not without a sanction. To be sure, in most circumstances it lacks a strong military sanction, especially when the aggressor is a great power; and any military provision for collective security is certainly not in sight at this time. However, the restraint is in fact produced by sanctions of sorts, both international and national. What are they and what is their effectiveness?

In the event of flagrant aggression, not only may allies come to the aid of the nation under attack, but possibly also other countries may choose to give support in one form or another; a great power may intervene, and various pressures may be organized under the auspices of the United Nations. In many, if not most, instances, nothing more may happen than an adverse reaction of "world public opinion." But is this of import? One hears, especially in the United States, frequent sneering references to "world public opinion" as something that is either fictitious or of no account. Such sneers are inspired by a profound misconception about international life.

INTERNATIONAL "COMMUNITY" AND WORLD OPINION

Admittedly, one also encounters views that greatly exaggerate the weight of world public opinion, and it is not easy to steer one's appraisal between these extreme estimates, for opinion is an elusive phenomenon, hard to measure and to trace in its consequences. World opinion would be a powerful force if, first, the world were highly integrated politically and, second, political opinions were substantially unified. Neither of these conditions prevails at this time. There *may be* a development under way that, as we suggested in the foregoing part of this chapter, will eventuate in firmer norms and more effective institutions for the control of interstate violence. But the extent to which mankind is at this time integrated politically can be easily overestimated.

One historian sees a trend toward some kind of "global cosmopolitanism" starting and growing over "the debris of older, parochial civilizations" as early as the 1850's.[34] There is an element of truth in this finding. There certainly has been a progressive enfeeblement of parochial values and identifications, for a century or so, stimulated by the robust onsweep of Western technological, scientific, and political ideas. It is also obvious that advancing Western technology and investment have caused an "information explosion," facilitating a rapid gathering, processing, and diffusion of information and, as a result, have brought about a highly interconnected world. Increased travel and study abroad have been augmenting cultural contacts; and there is now a greater abundance and use of international organizations—especially the United Nations and its specialized agencies—and of regional organizations as well, affording plenty of forums for international debate. It is therefore not exactly farfetched for some observers to discern the beginnings of a "world culture," mostly

[34] McNeill, *The Rise of the West*, pp. 727f.

evolving out of Europe, and informed by Western science and the West's rational view of government.[35] The power of these Western concepts has been great. One set, guiding human control over physical nature, is well understood; the other set, asserting that human institutions are man-made and hence subject to revision by human fiat, may in the end prove equally influential. As we suggested above, the spread and progress of industrialism and economic wealth seem to breed social goals and preferences that may issue in a universal attachment to such vague, but nonetheless significant, values as human welfare and dignity, and perhaps peace and security. There surely seems to be an incipient internationalization of some such concepts and expectations. It is indeed possible that a "world political culture is in the making,"[36] and it may be true that intellectuals the world over are carriers of this movement and, in some sense, are now participating in a world community of political ideas.[37]

Yet even if these assertions are perceptive and true, they do not mean that the world is politically integrated at this time. To be sure, politically sensitive men realize the extent to which nations have become interdependent, even though, in some respects—for example, the network of international trade—interdependence has tended to decline.[38] However, this more acute sense of international interdependence is largely engendered by

[35] Lucian W. Pye, "The Foreign Aid Instrument: Search for Reality," in Roger Hilsman and Robert C. Good (eds.), Foreign Policy in the Sixties, Baltimore: Johns Hopkins Press, 1965, p. 110.

[36] Gabriel A. Almond and Sidney Verba, The Civic Culture, Princeton: Princeton University Press, 1963, p. 4.

[37] Edward Shils, "The Intellectuals in the Political Development of the New States," World Politics, XII (April 1960), p. 348.

[38] Kenneth N. Waltz, "Contention and Management in International Relations," World Politics, XVII (July 1965), pp. 735ff.

political division and military risk. Intelligent observers are bound to recognize that political events in one country may have profound effects in others; that what happens in national politics anywhere, not just in a neighboring country, is therefore of great concern to governments elsewhere; and that the linkages between national polities and the international system are thus more numerous, more complex, and more salient than they were half a century ago. There is more interpenetration of national politics in the world arena. Above all, there is the appalling possibility that war in this age may gravely imperil other than contiguous or regional nations. For one thing, as one scholar observed,[39] the market for security has become less localized than it used to be; for another, war beween the great powers could spell an unprecedented scale of destruction and prove enormously disruptive far beyond their own territories. There is, in a way, a "community of fear."[40]

Fear, however, is not bound to unite; it is apt to prove divisive; certainly this kind of interdependence may produce neither stability nor cooperation. It does not necessarily encourage that sharing of values, beliefs, and motives, that smooth interlocking of complementary roles and expectations, upon which a true community must be based. On the contrary, the present world is riven by deep political cleavages, and rent by hostile ideologies.[41] It is still largely heterogeneous in culture, far more so than the societies comprising relatively closed regional systems in former times, such as ancient Greece and medieval Europe; and it is segmented in terms of politics. The transnational links that have

[39] Modelski, "Agraria and Industria," *op.cit.*, p. 143.

[40] Waltz, "Contention and Management," *op.cit.*, p. 737.

[41] Cf. Gerald D. Berreman, "Fear Itself: An Anthropologist's View," *Bulletin of the Atomic Scientists*, November 1964, pp. 8-11.

emerged and multiplied form a predominantly divisive and competitive pattern. In short, a foundation for a unified and powerful world public opinion does not at present exist.

What then is "world public opinion" and how much is it worth? Defined abstractly, public opinion reflects the expressed opinions of persons possessing some influence in public life. As already intimated, the formation of world opinion—opinions that react to events the world over and are, in part and to a degree, interconnected—rests on a strong and expanding technological foundation. Communication time has shrunk amazingly; and a richly ramified network, although of very uneven density, stretches all over the globe. It is chiefly composed of mass media of information—newspapers, radio, and television; but, lest one exaggerate the importance of these impersonal media, one must also note the ease and increasing frequency of person-to-person, including face-to-face, communication. As a whole, the news media, moreover, do not exactly report information with a passion for objectivity. Not only do governments influence the dissemination of news, exercising tight control in Communist and many other countries, but there are also commercial reasons, especially market considerations, that generate a tendency to distort the news.[42]

The vulgar skeptic of world opinion begins with a concept postulating a unitary body of opinion to which everyone—all of mankind—contributes, and, having set up this straw man, has little trouble knocking it down. In fact, only a relatively small minority of mankind is informed, interested, and influential enough to engage in making significant opinion in their own countries, and occasionally beyond. The masses of populations do not

[42] Cf. Einar Östgaard, "Factors Influencing the Flow of News," *Journal of Peace Research*, No. 1 (1965), pp. 39-62.

ordinarily care much about world political events, and this indifference is especially pronounced in the less developed countries, where illiteracy is still widespread, information relatively inaccessible, and preoccupation with immediate personal and local problems paramount.[43]

It is the elites—the politically active, informed, and relevant strata in each society—that participate in world opinion. Intellectuals have become prominent in these groups, notably in the less developed countries and the new states. The reasons for their enhanced weight, and often strategically important position, are two. First, nearly all nations, and the world as a whole, are and have been for some time in the grip of rapid economic, social, political, and cultural change—involved, as some writers put it, in the accelerating process of "modernization." The speed and complexity of these unsettling transformations continuously and urgently press societies to adjust, and to find solutions to new problems. In this dynamic situation, traditional values are often irrelevant or obsolete, and traditional precepts and solutions inadequate, if not stultifying; the premium is on analytical and inventive minds unhampered by a strong attachment to tradition. Intellectuals are as a group equipped to satisfy this need. Secondly, intellectuals command the skill for, and enjoy, articulating their views; they are—*par excellence*—the core of "the talking classes."[44] Outside the West and Japan, moreover, the modernizing elites must necessarily be recruited largely from the expanding ranks of those trained in colleges

---

[43] Cf. Hadley Cantril and Lloyd A. Free, *Hopes and Fears for Self and Country*, Supplement to *American Behavioral Scientist*, VI (October 1962).

[44] J. F. S. Ross, *Parliamentary Representation*, New Haven: Yale University Press, 1944, p. 115.

and universities because there is little of the propertied middle class that, in the course of the nineteenth century, performed much of the modernizing function in Europe and North America.

Now, it is normal for public opinion to be more or less divided on almost any important international issue, within and among nations. There is thus no single world opinion, as there is no single national opinion, but rather various opinion sections that are conditioned by a number of possible factors: the interests and position peculiar to particular countries, the influence of government, party affiliation, class position, images of the outside world engendered by past experience, various "spectacles" which stereoptically distort the view, and so on.

From the viewpoint of any nation whose government has committed an "illegitimate" act—that is, has behaved in a manner to which a large proportion of attentive and influential publics are negatively sensitized, and which they are inclined to condemn—the world may be roughly divided into four parts, though it must be kept in mind that opinion in each part is apt to be divided to some extent and also that, in each, there will be variation in the intensity with which opinions are held. These parts are: hostile countries, neutral countries, allied countries, and the offending country itself.

Any harm conferred by adverse opinion is obviously small in the case of countries ordinarily hostile to the offending state. Thus, if this state were the United States at the present time, it could take for granted a hostile opinion reaction in Communist countries concerning any of our foreign policies, and rest assured that Communist diplomacy would diligently exploit the issue wherever possible in the rest of the world. However, even opinion in Communist countries should not be regarded with complete indifference on our part. Of course, Communist governments fully control their national news media, and it is known that no sensitive news may pass uncensored, or unmanipulated, through the Iron and the Bamboo curtains. But Communist rule does not preclude the existence of public opinion in the Communist countries. Many American visitors to the Soviet Union have reported that, though the bulk of the Soviet population favors socialism, subscribes to a Soviet patriotism, and regards the United States as an imperialist, adversary state, it feels a degree of friendship and admiration for Americans as people; a similar situation appears to exist in Poland, Hungary, Czechoslovakia, and Yugoslavia. It might therefore make a difference to longer-range relations between the United States and these countries if conspicuously illegitimate American acts changed the reported sentiment to intense feelings of contempt and hatred.

Opinion in countries that are neutral or non-aligned with respect to the perpetrator of a grossly illegitimate act may be very significant in its consequences. Again taking the United States as an example, we must remember that it is heavily involved competitively with Moscow and Peking in wooing the non-aligned countries in order to persuade their leaders either to commit themselves against Communist diplomacy or at least not to pass diplomatically, or head over heels, into the Communist camp. The present East-West conflict constitutes, after all, a political and ideological as well as a military confrontation. In this rivalry, the non-aligned nations have figured as "potential converts or defectors as well as potential allies, and this has meant that their susceptibilities must be much more carefully weighed than would be the case if nothing more were in question than the military strength they can contribute to either camp."[45] This involvement gives the uncommitted countries—and opinion in them—a kind of "floating vote"[46] of considerable consequence.

One should not overestimate the size and weight of this floating vote. It is not as if the governments of most so-called uncommitted states, and some of those precariously aligned, enjoyed extreme flexibility in switching allegiance or favors. Alignment and realignment are, after all, responsive to more or less deeply anchored domestic forces in each country. The foreign policies of these states are seldom wholly or even predominantly mercenary, especially in view of the spreading hold of nationalism. Furthermore, the governments of the United States and the Soviet Union have had enough sobering experiences to have learned something of the limits set to their influence in this respect; and whenever they try a policy of détente between themselves, bidding for influence on the foreign policy of other states has a tendency to diminish somewhat. Despite these qualifications, however, their underlying rivalry in world politics persists and tends to render the rivals aware of the possible costs of flying in the face of "world opinion."

The importance of opinion in allied nations should be apparent to all. A more interesting part of world opinion is opinion in the perpetrating country itself. "World" opinion is composed of foreign and domestic opinion. To the extent that participants in influential domestic opinion are aware of the illegitimate act of their government, that opinion may be troubled and divided; in part at least it may be openly critical of, and hostile to, the

[45] Coral Bell, "Non-Alignment and the Power Balance," *Survival*, v (November-December 1963), p. 254.
[46] *Ibid.*

government. Of all four publics, the domestic will often be the most important.

Still, even if this analysis is accepted, how important is world opinion? What sort of sanction is it capable of imposing? The indispensable prerequisite of restraint produced by world opinion is that the nation and government in question perceive or anticipate adverse opinion and that they are sensitive to its consequences. The effective weight of the sanction is evidently capable of great variation, depending on a host of circumstances. It is this variability which marks it with vast uncertainty, and which lends chance, vagueness, and relative weakness to the sanction.

In the event that adverse opinion turns out to be strong, the reality of its pressure is apt to be appreciated with great immediacy if a sizable proportion of domestic opinion shares in the reaction. Governments are rarely indifferent to a drop in national support, especially at a time of international crisis. The efficacy of adverse opinion abroad is less easy to grasp, even when it is deep, noisy, and articulate. Skeptics contend that world opinion, even when aroused to a high pitch, tends to subside quickly in the face of accomplished fact, and to forget easily as new events claim attention. Although there is considerable truth in this belittlement, history records numerous cases of efficacy when the illegitimate act was dramatic, and opinion sensitized by previous jarring experiences.

The Germans, for example, have several times encountered the wrath and suffered the fateful consequences of aroused opinion abroad. In 1914, the United Kingdom might not have entered World War I as soon as it did, had it not been for the storm of indignation loosed by Germany's contemptuous violation of Belgian neutrality; and the United States might not have entered that war, or entered when it did, without intense indignation over Germany's resort to unrestricted submarine war. Hitler's aggressive acts during the middle and late 1930's gradually alarmed a world loath to take up arms and prepared the way for the grand coalition that finally took the field against him. Nor can it be said that the memory of foreign opinion is always short. Here again, Germany is a good case in point. Even now, twenty years ater the end of World War II, Germans are aware of the frostiness, suspicion, and even rank hostility with which they are received in nations such as Norway, Denmark, and Great Britain.

But there are less dramatic, and yet serious, costs which adverse foreign opinion may impose on an offending nation. World opinion can be effective in subtle and cumulative ways. Nations have and require other bases than military power for international influence. As mentioned above, the on-going conflict between the United States and the Communist powers manifests itself primarily in a ceaseless competition for the allegiance or favor of other states, and it is mainly on this allegiance that the attitudes of influential groups toward the chief international actors exert their impact. Thus, if a state flagrantly flouts an internationally sanctioned restraint on military aggression, it may, in the event of success, gain the object of aggression and in addition perhaps inspire increased respect for its military prowess; but it may also tarnish its non-military reputation and provoke attitudes of suspicion and hostility that, over the longer run if not immediately, will become organized politically, and perhaps militarily as well. Figuratively speaking, it may win battles but lose the war. This amounts to saying that the respect a nation enjoys—respect for acting properly, with sensitivity to internationally widespread moral standards, and with sobriety and restraint in resorting to military power—is a precious asset in foreign affairs. It is an asset that assists in holding and gaining allies, and generally in promoting a favorable reception for its diplomatic initiatives. In this respect, international politics is no different from national politics. Success in politics depends considerably on how a person is able to relate himself to others, and an excessive power drive may impoverish this relationship by depriving it of elements of confidence, admiration, sympathy, and even affection from which much political influence may be derived. So it is with states in the international arena. Respect earned in, and bestowed by, the outside world is not an asset a government should be eager to squander.

Nor is adverse domestic opinion to be ignored. Modern governments command considerable means for manipulating domestic opinion and portraying their act as legitimate. But as the British reaction to the Suez venture in 1956 demonstrated dramatically, there are limits to this power to persuade, and hence to the ability of governments to ignore the opinion sanction. It is not only that any government prefers the widest possible support for its policies; in addition to the respect of the outside world, a nation also needs self-respect. To the extent that a nation recognizes an illegitimate act by its government, and to the extent that its public has internalized the norms on which legitimacy rests, it will suffer the costs, also internalized, of shame and deflated self-respect. To that extent, an accepted restraint is a self-denying ordinance.

In conclusion, it is the payment of these "costs" imposed by critical domestic and foreign opinion that a government will take into account, to the limit of its understanding of these intangible forces, when considering an illegitimate or doubtfully legitimate resort to military force. Admittedly, these costs are uncertain in advance, hard to estimate at the moment of decision and, besides, may fully accrue only over the longer run. As we also conceded, there may even be gains to be derived from the unconcerned and ruthless employment of illegitimate aggression—that is, from the inspiration abroad of fear and the exaction of supine compliance. Since the willingness of statesmen to accept the costs of illegitimate action is obviously sensitive to the value of the object at stake in the act, the restraint may be an insufficient deterrent when this value is large and prove to be more effective in crises with lesser implications. A nation confident in its military prowess may also be less prone to pay heed to foreign opinion than one whose military position is precarious; and—as is generally true of policy-making—governments may be misinformed, misjudge their environment, or act irrationally. In any case, however, there are costs. They may be substantial and sometimes formidable, especially when they accumulate over some time and when, at the moment of choosing policy, they seem outweighed by the prospective profits of malfeasance. And if our previous analysis is correct, if it is true that, with spreading and progressing "modernization," the influence of "publics" the world over tends to be on the rise, then these costs will have a tendency to increase in the future.

To be effective, this sanction of critical world opinion must ultimately find expression in the self-restraint of states; and states obviously vary both in the sensitivity with which opinion publics watch their behavior, and in the degree to which their leaders are willing to take this opinion into account. World opinion tends to be especially sensitive to the behavior of the great powers; and, at this stage, anyhow, opinion outside the West is, for reasons of past experience, particularly sensitive to the behavior of the Western nations. Indonesia can get by with actions which, if undertaken by Britain or the United States, would inflame world opinion. On the other hand, states tend to be self-restrained in proportion to the international assets that their governments expect to lose if they brusquely defy world opinion, or which they know they stand to gain if they "display a decent respect for the opinions of mankind." If people in the United States are at present peculiarly apt to chafe under this restraint, and even to scoff at "world public opinion," this is probably due to the fact that, on both counts, the United States finds itself uniquely "on the spot" because resentment focuses easily on a dominant power, and because public opinion is of more account in the mid-twentieth century than it was in the eighteenth and nineteenth centuries, when France and Great Britain respectively were predominant powers. The United States thus finds foreign opinion highly sensitive to its acts, and dares not be indifferent to its actual or potential pressure even when that pressure is deemed to be unjust or "opinionated."

What, finally, can the historical record tell us about the effectiveness of world public opinion in deterring military aggression? It cannot tell us much, chiefly because we know little about illegitimate acts considered but, after consideration, forgone by governments; and because other pressures and motivations were usually at work when a negative decision was made or when an aggressive enterprise was called off, as in the case of the Suez crisis of 1956. (Whether or not, or the extent to which, the military actions of Britain, France, and Israel constituted aggression is a very controversial question.) It may be significant, however, that despite numerous violent conflicts since 1945, there has been no declaration of war; and virtually all of these conflicts were either short-lived and sporadic border conflicts in which the "aggressor" was notoriously hard to identify, or—being uprisings against a colonial power or arising in connection with internal rebellions and revolutions—could claim exemption on grounds of constituting "wars of liberation."

To mention a few specific examples, India's seizure of Goa was regarded by a large proportion of world opinion as a legitimate act of freeing a colonial population. The Korean war started as an "internal war." Chinese attacks on the "offshore islands" are of a doubtfully aggressive nature, since many people consider these islands, and Taiwan, as belonging rightfully to China. China's military action against India in 1962 was in the nature of a spectacular border clash. The military intervention by the Soviet Union in suppressing the Hungarian uprising in 1956 incited strong condemnation abroad and might have provoked more if it had not been diverted in large part by the simultaneous events of the Suez crisis.

There is no doubt that several military actions undertaken by the United States since World War II have touched off adverse opinion in many parts of the world, not only in Communist states, but also in the non-aligned countries and among its allies. This certainly happened in the case of the ill-fated invasion of Cuba in 1961, in which the United States government was a confessed accomplice; it happened when the United States intervened militarily in the Dominican Republic in 1965; and it happened as the United States became more deeply involved militarily in the South Vietnamese civil war and initiated limited military attacks on North Vietnam. If these military actions aroused a great deal of critical and hostile opinion abroad, as well as in the United States itself, this was partly for reasons discussed in the previous section of this chapter. But it happened also because, as already mentioned, the United States seems to be at the present time a target especially attractive to critical world opinion. This is again an example of the complex conditionality of the problems examined in this essay. It certainly looks at times as if the "opinion elites" apply a double standard, and expect more virtue from the United States than from the Soviet Union, mainland China, or most other nations. This poses a special problem for the United States. It is as if this country were made to walk a tightrope. On the one hand, if it does not want to be immobilized by the restraining hands of friends and allies, not to mention the uncommitted nations, it must rebuff the counsel of inaction, proceed to act whenever the stake is indubitably important, and stand prepared to shoulder some costs in terms of adverse opinion. On the other hand, the American people can also feel pride in the fact that so much of the world expects the United States to behave with more propriety, and more moral sensibility, than it expects others to display. This special expectation reflects a respect which is not only an international asset but should also justify an incremental measure of self-respect. And it might well be claimed, furthermore, that the long-term interests of the United States are best served by a world order in which all governments are increasingly prepared to honor legitimacy, and that the chances of bringing about such an international order are improved by steadfast American example.

ANOTHER INCREASED COST OF CONQUEST

The exceedingly variable, uncertain, vague, and not usually strong sanction that world public opinion may impose on a state ignoring the reduction in the legitimacy of international war is not the only condition that, compared with the past, inflates the costs of territorial conquest. Until not long ago, conquest was usually cheap, in the sense that the conquered population submitted to the fiat of arms and caused little trouble for the conquering state. This was generally the case in European history, when provinces changed hands with great frequency—at least until in the nineteenth century the sway of popular nationalism, a novel political force, made conquered populations sullen, intractable, and given to irredentist activity. It was Napoleon who encountered guerrilla war—then a new phenomenon in Europe—in Iberia and in the Austrian Tirol. Following defeat, if there was any military resistance, submission to the conqueror was also the rule as European nations acquired overseas colonies.

Such submissiveness cannot be expected in the present world, which is sensitized to the injustice of imperialism and solidly dedicated to the idea of self-determination and self-rule. Despite one bloody uprising, it was not hard for Great Britain to rule Egypt for many decades before World War I. But one wonders what the British and French would have done in 1956 had they occupied Egypt. Even if they had decisively beaten Nasser's regular forces, in all likelihood they would have failed to organize a viable alternative government—a "puppet" government, as it would have been branded inevitably—and would have faced interminable irregular warfare and terrorism. Surely, the French learned in Indo-China and Algeria that to rule a recalcitrant population, determined to gain independence, is extremely costly and, indeed, infeasible—especially since any group suffering under a foreign oppressor can now count on ample support from the outside world.

In this respect, too, world politics has undergone rapid and momentous change. That change was highly visible during World War II when the Nazi conquerors were everywhere challenged by civilian resistance movements, in Russia and the Ukraine, in Yugoslavia and Greece, in France and Norway; and after that war it was equally visible in Kenya and Algeria. The simple fact is that foreign rule by force of arms is no longer tolerable, and is universally regarded as illegitimate. Any ruling nation is bound to discover that the military, political, and moral costs have mounted to a level far above what they used to be until a few decades ago. They are now a drain, making territorial conquest unprofitable and unattractive.

The incidence of this factor, however, will vary with the identity, as a type, of the conqueror and the conquered. Postwar experience indicates that the costs of occupying and administrating conquered territory tends to be greater when the occupying power is Western and wealthy, and the occupied territory is non-Western and poor, than when both are in the second category. Occupation by Western powers seems to trigger special reactions formed and nurtured during the era of Western colonialism. On the other hand, the costs of occupying and administering new territory might be less for underdeveloped states, or perceived by the governments to be less, both in terms of their capacity to aid the occupied population and the expectations of the occupied.

THE DAVID AND GOLIATH ACT

Turning to political conflicts between militarily strong and weak nation-states, one is impressed by the remarkable success with which, during the last two decades, weak powers have defied big powers. For instance, though greatly varying in size, China, Yugoslavia, and Albania are all decidedly inferior in military strength to the Soviet Union, and yet have defied the latter successfully. Similarly, Cuba and North Vietnam have defied the United States, and Egypt has defied Britain and France. And on a level of less intense crisis, it has become common for militarily weak governments—such as those of Ghana or Tanzania, Algeria or Indonesia—to undertake, or tolerate on their territory, expressions of hostility or contempt, verbal or otherwise, against big powers—acts that, before World War I or II, would have been considered intolerably offensive and would have led to drastic and effective reprisals. In no particular event has the outcome of such squabbles, disputes, or crises reflected the balance of military power. Indeed, as Aron observes, never has it been more difficult for the strong to impose their will on the weak.[47]

There seems to be no fully satisfactory explanation for this remarkable phenomenon; and the best I can offer is unsure speculation and untested hypotheses. We must not hasten to conclude that this phenomenon is to be explained entirely, or perhaps even primarily, by a sharply diminished importance of military power as a regulator of international behavior. Apart from the existence of nuclear weapons—discussion of which has been reserved for Chapters IV and V, and which have little, if any, bearing on the problem—six considerations may contribute to an understanding of why the David and Goliath act is so popular, and apparently riskless.

One explanation points to the intense competition between the United States and the Soviet Union for international influence, and the guardianship which these two great powers have assumed over many allies and client states. Great power rivalry has induced the United States on many an occasion to pay blackmail to a government threatening to move its country into align-

[47] *Paix et guerre*, p. 436.

ment with Communist states; and the Soviet Union has certainly had similar experiences. As this rivalry engenders fat concessions to neutral states, so it also produces in the great powers a special care to refrain from taking offense easily at the provocative behavior of small states, and occasionally to absorb silently ignominious abuse. Moreover, when defying one big power, many, if not most, militarily weak states have, or count on, diplomatic and perhaps military backing from the other great power. Since, for reasons indicated in the next chapter, the two great powers are not anxious to confront each other in a serious crisis, the mere likelihood that such backing will be forthcoming suffices to permit many a successful act of defiance. For the bearded power, the stake involved in any squabble or dispute with a defiant small power is usually too low to warrant counteractions that risk bringing about a critical confrontation with the other great power. To the extent that this factor is operative, we must of course conclude, not that military power has lost potency in international affairs, but that the possible interposition of large counterpower curbs its exertion.

Second, the successful David and Goliath act seems to reflect another change in moral temper. To some extent, this is not a question of the strong finding it harder than ever to impose his will on the weak, but of the stronger not caring to impose his will under circumstances in which this was customary in the past. The UN Charter and the debates in that institution give vent to a strongly egalitarian concept of nationhood. According to this concept, states have internationally equal rights to integrity, safety, and—one supposes—freedom of speech, regardless of size, wealth, or military strength. This notion rests on a moral foundation which is now fairly widespread throughout the world. It is found not only in many of the small new states—some of which have developed considerable *amour-propre* and delight in exercising their rights at the slightest opportunity—but also, more or less, in the large and militarily superior states. Goliath has become somewhat more civilized. To the extent that this new moral value gives rise to a permissiveness for which former and more rank-conscious ages were not known, military might has lost usefulness for this particular purpose.

To these two factors, which go far toward explaining the diminished relevance of even gross differences in military power in the relationships of states, must be added, third, the condition described earlier—namely the diminished legitimacy, or the illegitimacy, of displaying military power except in defense against aggression or for the liberation of oppressed peoples. A fourth factor is harder to describe and evaluate but also seems very important. Most of the militarily weak states are economically underdeveloped and inhabited by non-white populations, many of which were until recently ruled as colonies by economically more developed states that, with few exceptions, were "capitalist" and inhabited by populations of white complexion. As a result of this historical experience, there are today among influential people throughout most of Asia and Africa, and in Latin America as well, diffuse but substantial feelings of fear and distrust of the Western powers. This is a reservoir of sentiment which the Communists, and lately especially the government of Communist China, seek assiduously to preserve, magnify, and exploit. At the present time, this sentiment is easily focused on the United States, the leading "capitalist" state and militarily the most powerful Western country, which, moreover, maintains concrete displays of this military power far beyond its boundaries, in most parts of the world.

Fifth, as discussed earlier, there is the new militant nationalism that is now spreading through the non-Western world, and that renders territorial conquest a prohibitively expensive enterprise. The very difficulty which the United States is experiencing in South Vietnam indicates that even the most sophisticated paraphernalia of military power afford scant political leverage when application "runs counter to the tide of a country's nationalism."[48] Finally, and related to the fifth point, the military forces of the two superpowers are largely structured in relation to one another. They are huge and incredibly complex, capable of meting out destruction on a scale grotesquely disproportionate to what would be appropriate for chastening a small and weak country, and in a sense, because of its very sophistication, ill-adapted to coping with men armed merely with simple rifles and hand grenades, able to do without highways and to hide in the jungle.

These factors should go far toward explaining the curious ability of the Davids to challenge the Goliaths. It is in part that the Goliaths do not care for moral reasons to exploit their military superiority; it is largely that the costs of wielding military power are too high in these confrontations in which little is to be gained. There is therefore a gap between the power a state is equipped to exercise and the power it has the incentive to exercise. This leads naturally to an appreciation of the power of the less powerful,[49] and hence the small powers are weak but not meek. The great powers are induced to take special care, at the present time, not to appear to

[48] George McT. Kahin and John W. Lewis, "The United States in Vietnam," *Bulletin of the Atomic Scientists*, June 1965, p. 37.

[49] For a similar analysis, see Karl W. Deutsch, *The Nerves of Government*, New York: Free Press, 1963, p. 115; Dahl, *Modern Political Analysis*, pp. 47ff.

act as a military bully, or as a "white" power contemptuous of the sovereignty of non-white and ex-colonial populations—*pace* "world public opinion."

This diminished usability of military strength by great powers against small and weak states is of great significance. During the past hundred years, great powers have been reluctant to wage war against one another. They did so, of course, in World Wars I and II. But between 1871 and 1914, and between 1918 and 1939, though there were many wars they did not involve the confrontation of great powers. They were wars between small powers, such as the Balkan wars of the pre-1914 era, or they pitted a great power against a small power, as in the cases of the British-Afghan war of 1878, the Boer War of 1899-1902, or—following World War I—the war of Italy against Ethiopia, Japan's war against China, and Russia's war against Finland in 1939. And there were many more cases—when gunboat diplomacy was still frequently practiced—of a great power sending out an expeditionary force against a greatly inferior country.

The upshot of the new conditions examined in this chapter is fairly clear. To the extent that leaders perceive them, they act as restraints on the employment and the employability of military power. On these several accounts, military power has appreciably lost in political utility, compared with preceding ages. For a considerable range of foreign policy purposes, military superiority is now at a discount.

CHAPTER IV

THE GREAT NUCLEAR POWERS

THE PRECEDING CHAPTER discussed some "costs," and hence restraints, on the use of national military power as if nuclear arms did not exist. But these restraints, though now of greater magnitude and impact than they were even three decades ago, are precipitants of social, economic, and political forces that have been operating over a considerable past, and that would have generated these effects even if nuclear weaponry had not been invented. They are connected with the development of modern science and technology, and the progressive industrialization and economic development of human societies. Nuclear armaments, and the particular restraints on the employment of military power that their characteristics stimulated, are also, of course, a product and result of modern science and technology. But they are a precipitant more recent in origin.

As suggested in Chapter I, if we are interested in changes in the utility of military power, we are concerned with the utility of international war, the utility of military threats, and the utility derived from the mere possession of military forces. These distinctions serve a purpose since, although the different kinds of utilities are obviously related, any changes in the utility of military power need not produce equal changes in the other utilities. Unhappily for the purpose of clear exposition, all these utilities are a function of many variable factors, and concentration on any one runs the danger of seemingly ignoring or belittling the others. Thus, any one of the utilities is a function (1) of how the military capabilities of possible opponents compare quantitatively and qualitatively in military effectiveness; (2) of the stakes involved in a clash of interests; (3) of the skill of statesmen and military leaders; (4) of the propensity of governments and generals to accept risks and to behave rationally; (5) of the character and strength of domestic political support; and (6) of moral, political, and legal restraints. But they are also a function of what concerns us at this point—namely, the properties of military technology. Focusing now on this factor, we may argue as follows: If, as a general phenomenon in the international system, the utility of international war rose or declined, one would logically expect the utility of military threats and of military capabilities to change in the same direction, and this especially if one disregards, as this essay does, the domestic uses of military forces. After all, a threat would be useless if the flat disutility of proceeding to war were known to all parties concerned; and the mere possession of armed forces is useful as long as they are usable—that is, if they enable a government to utter a threat or counterthreat, or to precipitate or join in war. It is on this usability of military forces, and the anticipation that they may be used, that their value rests. However, even if—as a result of changes in military technology—the several utilities change in the same direction, these changes tend not to be proportionate. Thus, if the utility of resorting to war declines as a result of technological factors, the utility of threats will tend to decline less, since the threatening party need not be compelled to make good its threat and since the recipient of a threat may not be sure whether the threatening government is purely bluffing or apt to behave irrationally. The utility derived from the mere possession of armed forces should also decline less, since the potential threat or counterthreat implicit in the possession of armed forces produces this value without the disadvantage attached to an explicit threat—namely, that an unheeded threat may compel the threatening power to choose between executing the threatening action or having its threat revealed as a bluff.

THE NEW MILITARY TECHNOLOGY

We have said, and must reiterate, that observable shifts in the utility of national military power—and changes in the usability of military forces—make it clear that these effects are highly sensitive to variable conditions. The form of military force is one of these conditions. As we all know, the emergence of nuclear weapons—by which we mean nuclear explosives, associated delivery vehicles, and supporting infrastructure—has had a truly revolutionary impact on the nature of armed conflict and, indeed, on the nature of military security. It has sharply impinged on the usability of military capabilities, primarily as the result of five properties and consequences.

First is the enormous increase in the scale of destruction. One should not forget, to be sure, that scientific and technological advance, and the ability of industrial nations to pour huge amounts of capital into the military sector, had been rapidly increasing the destructiveness of weapons for some time. The devastation visited on Germany in World War II was unprecedented in terms of previous experience; and, had nuclear arms not been introduced, weapons of greater destructive power would no doubt have been developed in any case. However, the destructive capacity of nuclear weaponry represents a revolutionary progression; it involves a "quantum jump" of stupendous and awesome proportions. The two nuclear superpowers possess the means to snuff out human life on a gigantic, if not exhaustive, scale.

Second, there is at present the enormous technological superiority of offensive over defensive forces. Although the offensive has enjoyed technological superiority over the defensive at various times in the past, such superiority was not coupled with the immense destructive power now available. Over the hundred or so years preceding 1945, defensive weaponry was technologically somewhat superior to offensive arms, so that offensive victory was usually the fruit of great superiority in numbers, tactical surprise, vastly better generalship or morale, or was achieved at the expense of disproportionately large casualties.

The decisive domination of the offense that prevails at the present time has made the nation-state, and especially its population and accumulated wealth, strikingly more vulnerable than was the case before. According to the brilliant analysis of John Herz, the very *raison d'être* of the nation-state resided in its ability to lend military protection and security to the population it encompassed by surrounding itself with a "hard shell" of armies and fortifications that were effective in obstructing foreign penetration into the "soft interior," and thus afforded a basic "impermeability."[50] As Herz notes, this impermeability began, in fact, to diminish as—with increasing economic development and international economic specialization—the nation-state became, at least for a time, less self-sufficient and thus vulnerable to economic blockade in time of war. The new trend toward "total war" observable during World War I, which led to civilians being regarded as legitimate objects of warfare by means of economic blockade, exploited this vulnerability; and with the development of efficient aircraft, "the roof blew off the territorial state,"[51] as World War II amply demonstrated. This development has now culmi-

[50] John H. Herz, *International Politics in the Atomic Age*, New York: Columbia University Press, 1959, pp. 40f.
[51] *Ibid.*, p. 104.

nated in the huge destructiveness of nuclear explosives, against which, so far at least, there is no effective defense affording protection to territories and populations. The "hard shell" of the nation-state has been shattered and, as Herz suggests, the age of "territoriality" has passed. The classic nation-state has perhaps lost its principal *raison d'être*.[52] Today it looks as if unlimited might is associated with absolute impotence.[53] If and to the extent that this is true, military superiority has ceased to be meaningful, and it will remain so as long as offensive forces retain the towering dominance they have achieved as a result of the number and relative invulnerability of nuclear weapons, the speed with which attack can be launched and consummated, and the unlimited choice of targets available to the attacker.

The third characteristic concerns the greatly enhanced uncertainties about the capabilities of military forces and about international relationships of military power—coupled as these uncertainties are with the certitude of immense destructiveness. Nations lack experience with the strategic and tactical use of sophisticated nuclear weapons, and governments disposing of nuclear armament are today far less knowledgeable than they were before the nuclear age about the military effectiveness of their own armed forces and especially about those of their prospective opponents. Not surprisingly, the experts are setting more store by gaming exercises. War gaming has acquired greater conceptual refinement and uses the new powerful tool of the electronic computer. Yet the results of simulation are necessarily sensitive to the design of programs. The good design presupposes an input of knowledge that is hard to come by, harder to validate, and incapable of commanding full confidence.

[52] *Ibid.*, pp. 5, 42.
[53] *Ibid.*, p. 169.

The decrease in military knowledge stems chiefly from the fact that highly qualitative technical features of increasingly sophisticated nuclear weapons, delivery mechanisms and facilities for command and control have become crucially important to their functioning; that the pursuit of the technological arms race leads to the continuous "improvement" and change of these features; and that their design is readily surrounded by a wall of secrecy. In consequence, international differences in military capabilities are much harder to estimate, and the outcome of any future contest of arms has become more chancy than used to be the case.

To be sure, military power has never been easy to measure, and international differences in military strength were therefore always difficult to calculate and easy to misapprehend. In addition to constituents that could be counted readily—battleships, regiments, and guns—there were always the imponderables of qualitative differences in generalship and troop morale, and the possible intervention of accidental conditions, such as weather and disease. Nor were generals free from ignorance and often grossly mistaken ideas about the implications of new weaponry. Before 1914, for instance, Marshall Foch based his famous and fatal strategy of *l'offensive à l'outrance* on the flat assumption, subsequently proven wrong, that all improvements in firearms added to the strength of the offensive.[54]

But the problem of calculating and comparing military power has now become still more difficult. Who, for example, can trust his imagination to foresee the pace of battle fought with tactical nuclear weapons on both sides? Moreover, the problem has become more important as the consequences of a mistaken estimate have grown

[54] This point and the example have been called to my attention by Professor Norman Gibbs of Oxford University.

more fatal. Error was more tolerable when war was—for technological as well as political reasons—less destructive of civilian populations and more limited in its consequences; decisions to go to war were more readily made. Today, the consequences of error have become dire. The uncertainties make any but the grossest known imbalances in military strength a dubious basis for military planning and high decisions of states. Technical military uncertainties are thus compounded by uncertainty about what hostile governments—facing doubts and the colossal risks of a false step—will choose to do in an emergency. Finally, should belligerents blunder into all-out nuclear war, they might be unable to end the war fast enough to prevent mutual mass destruction. These various uncertainties, in fact, contribute appreciably to deterring any decision to precipitate war.

Fourth, there is the dramatically increased, and indeed global, reach of nuclear weaponry. Nuclear warheads capable of delivery by long-range aircraft, intercontinental rockets, and roaming ships can be launched against targets anywhere on the globe, and exploded on target with great dispatch. Until these appalling weapons appeared on the scene, the military power of a nation inevitably declined as it moved away from its home base. The cost of transmitting power over space, this "loss-of-strength gradient,"[55] is still effective for conventional— that is, non-nuclear and non-strategic—forces; and, to that extent, geography and distance remain important. If nuclear weapons are not available or usable, it still makes a big difference to military operations that Korea is a peninsula and Taiwan an island—and both therefore subject to the influence of sea power, with its relatively

[55] Kenneth E. Boulding, *Conflict and Defense: A General Theory*, New York: Harper, 1962, pp. 230ff. See also Modelski, "Agraria and Industria," *op.cit.*, p. 133.

low transportation costs—that South Vietnam has a very long coastline, and that Manchuria, the main area of China's industrial war potential, is far from South Vietnam. But as far as long-range nuclear weapons are concerned, the cost of transmitting military power has fallen dramatically. In this respect, too, the world has "shrunk." Against a nuclear great power there is no safety anywhere.

Finally, there is the fabulous speed with which nuclear weapons can reach their targets. This also represents an important difference between the present and the pre-nuclear past. Although the phenomenon of the *Blitzkrieg* has been observable through the ages, armies and navies were cumbersome and slow; belligerents relied on the mobilization of additional military strength while hostilities were in progress; and war was therefore ordinarily slow in gathering momentum. This ponderousness gave governments time to consider and reconsider, especially when war had been precipitated by mistake, and enabled them to negotiate its end before destruction reached too large a scale. This potential margin of security may have gone, or at least become much less reliable, with the advent of nuclear armament.

All five changes tend to restrict, singly and together, the usability and hence the political utility of national military power in various ways. Their overall impact is indeed easy to perceive. However, in order to improve our understanding of these developments, and their consequences, we must once again note how they vary with circumstance.

THE CONFRONTATION OF THE SUPERPOWERS

As between the two major nuclear powers, the strategic nuclear weapons of each are capable of visiting quick and enormous destruction on the civilian populations of the other. Adequate defenses do not at present exist, if by "adequate" we mean defenses capable of reducing casualties to a magnitude approaching the levels sustained by Germany, Japan, and the Soviet Union during the Second World War. The United States is at present following a policy aimed at damage limitation, in the event of strategic war, as well as one aimed at deterring attack. However, according to Mr. McNamara, the Secretary of Defense, this country would suffer civilian casualties numbered in the tens of millions if the Soviet Union were to launch a large-scale and efficient attack and did not go out of its way to minimize the destruction of cities. "Damage limitation" apparently cannot prevent catastrophic damage. The present position of the USSR is estimated to be no better, and almost certainly is appreciably worse. Nor can civilian populations at this time receive adequate protection by the execution of a pre-emptive strike against the opponent's attack forces. The "survivability" which missile launchers have acquired by means of hardening, dispersion, mobility, concealment, and sheer numbers discourages pre-emption. In the pre-nuclear age, a state was unable to inflict such an enormous degree of damage before it had defeated the opponent's armed forces and, after victory, it had normally no cause to inflict such damage, since the vanquished power gave in. The war was over. As long as the outcome of battle was sufficiently indeterminate, as it frequently was, and military defeat uncertain, the risk of war was often accepted; that is, the value at stake in international conflict seemed to justify acceptance of the estimated consequences of hostilities. The prospects of large-scale nuclear war are utterly different now that the offense has an overwhelming advantage over defensive forces.

As long as these conditions—the conditions of the

mutual balance of terror—prevail, it is hard to think of conflict objectives valuable enough to justify the deliberate initation of large-scale nuclear war. The disproportion between the military means and any conceivable foreign-policy objective is so vast that such an act would be irrational. It is true, of course, that deterrence depends, strictly speaking, not only on the devastation an attacking nation must expect to absorb but also on the gains expected from nuclear war. As long as both antagonists must expect to suffer enormous damage, however, no conceivable gains could offset or exceed the losses, and self-deterrence results unless irrationality intervenes. Under this condition, it is widely deduced, the threat of precipitating such a war for the purpose of enforcing foreign-policy demands on a major nuclear power is bound to lack credibility. It is not surprising that Herman Kahn speaks of a widespread feeling of "nuclear incredulity."[56]

In terms of the national effort expended on them, strategic nuclear forces are certainly very important military capabilities maintained in the United States and the Soviet Union. Military forces of this importance have in the past served as a useful instrument in the pursuit of a wide range of foreign-policy objectives. However, strategic nuclear forces do not command this broad and diffuse usefulness. This does not mean, of course, that they lack utility from the viewpoint of one nuclear power confronting another. But their usefulness is narrow and specific, for it rests primarily on the ability to deter nuclear attack. Now that nuclear arms exist, this deterrent value may afford the leaders of the major nuclear powers utility as great as, or greater than, the utility that military power has ever offered to political leaders. What we are

[56] Herman Kahn, *On Escalation: Metaphors and Scenarios*, New York: Praeger, 1965, p. 89.

compelled to deduce, however, is that strategic nuclear forces do not have the *scope* of usefulness that non-nuclear powers possessed in the past.

Moreover, the existence of strategic nuclear weapons casts a shadow on the value of hypothetical limited conflicts in which strategic weapons are not employed. Any limited conflict—for instance, a conventional war—between nuclear powers carries the risk of escalating to the strategic level at which, as long as the mutual balance of terror prevails, the pay-offs are hugely negative for both contestants. The risk of *deliberate* escalation may be small, if not infinitesimal, under these conditions; the risk of *inadvertent* escalation may be greater. To the extent that this risk inhibits lesser military conflict between nuclear powers, the existence of strategic nuclear weapons also reduces the scope of useful purposes to which limited-war capabilities, especially non-nuclear forces, may be put. The risk of the inadvertent outbreak of strategic nuclear war, while the balance of terror prevails, is hard to estimate; and when the consequences involved are so fatal, even a small risk is a serious matter. In the pre-nuclear past, certainly, war has often come about by mistake. World War I was in 1914 unpremeditated by all major governments involved; and in 1939, Hitler did not expect his aggressive moves to entail the large-scale prolonged war which World War II became. Such precedents would be ominous indeed were it not for the fact that the governments of the two superpowers are keenly aware of this danger and utterly determined to escape it. This is part of the self-deterrence which is implicit in mutual deterrence. As a result, these governments treat each other with great circumspection when entangled in a serious crisis.

The two governments acted with such caution in the several crises in and over Berlin. In each case the Soviet government, which initiated these crises, increased the pressure step by cautious step, taking discriminating care that no new move was apt to provoke a violent response. By using the government of the German Democratic Republic for implementing many of the moves—a classical example of acting by proxy—the Soviet Union left itself avenues for retreat that it could tread without intolerable loss of face; and in each instance the Soviet Union eventually withdrew from its extreme demand and accepted a compromise. Again, both governments exhibited exemplary prudence when they confronted one another in the course of the Cuban missiles crisis in 1962. Though we know nothing about the deliberations that took place in the Kremlin, the record of Khrushchev's acts and his communications to President Kennedy give evidence of the care he took to prevent a further intensification of the crisis. On the American side, several firsthand accounts of the labors in the White House have been made public. They disclose the most painstaking dedication to prudence and restraint, even though the government was staunchly determined to have the Soviet missiles removed from Cuban soil.[57] It can also be taken for granted that both powers have taken utmost care to prevent the sort of failure in command and control that figures so luridly in fictional accounts of how a future nuclear war might break out.

And yet the inadvertent precipitation of nuclear war remains a substantial risk. One crisis, or even several crises, well managed do not insure that every crisis will subside or be terminated without a fatal misstep. Governments *are* capable of blunder; and, after all, Khrushchev evidently acted on a serious miscalculation of likely United States reactions when he authorized Soviet

[57] Cf. Theodore C. Sorensen, "Kennedy vs. Khrushchev: The Showdown in Cuba," *Look*, September 7, 1965, pp. 43-54.

missiles to be emplaced in Cuba. Risks are hard to calculate. As we shall develop below, communication may well fail at the critical moment; an actor may be tempted to sail too close to the wind in pressing his opponent; the assumption of perfect rationality is not calculated to dissipate worry; and too often in the human situation events dominate intentions.

Thus, against whatever utility nuclear powers derive from their ability to deter strategic war and, to a lesser extent, limited war between one another must be set the *disutility* that general war, which it is in the strongest interest of each to avoid, may nevertheless occur by mistake or accident. The proponents of disarmament are aware of this. They are convinced that this situation puts a premium on greater human wisdom, rationality, and restraint, on safer containment of imprudence, passion, and stupidity, than past governments have been able to muster over any length of time. To the disarmer, national armaments evidently represent a net disutility.

However, the conclusion so far reached calls for refinement. Several qualifications come to mind. First, nuclear weapons are not, of course, all alike in purpose, explosive yield, and other relevant properties. At least by objective standards, they differ in the threatened scale of destruction, and should also differ in their escalatory potential. Might they not also differ in usability, and hence in utility? For instance, how do essentially defensive systems such as atomic demolition munitions and antisubmarine and anti-aircraft weapons, with nuclear warheads, differ in the threatened scale of destruction from similar non-nuclear weapons? If a bridge is destroyed by a nuclear demolition charge, and a submarine sunk or an aircraft shot down by means of a nuclear explosive, no more destruction has taken place than if non-nuclear ammunition had been used, except for the effects of a small amount of radioactive fall-out, and that can be minimized by proper design of the explosive and a judicious choice of yield. And, are certain "clean" tactical nuclear weapons of very small yield not simply accomplishing a given destructive mission more economically, in terms of delivery effort, than a larger mass of conventional explosives? Are nuclear weapons detonated over one's own territory as escalatory as such weapons exploded on the territory of an adversary? Will even one strategic nuclear weapon, fired in order to symbolize resolve in an intense crisis—perhaps while a local military conflict is in process—and with due care to minimize or avoid damage, necessarily touch off a large-scale exchange involving disaster on both sides?

These questions cannot be answered now, at least with anything approaching confidence. What matters here is not so much that weapons and modes of employing them differ appreciably by objective standards, as how the governments of the great nuclear powers structure their perceptions and responses; and this would seem to depend upon whether or not opponents agree—either at the time of crisis or beforehand, and either tacitly or formally—that these distinctions are relevant and should guide their conflict behavior. Whether this agreement will occur or not, we do not know at this time. However, if it did come about, such agreement would tend to make nuclear weapons of some types, or in particular forms of employment, more widely usable—that is to say, extend their utility beyond the narrow range likely to obtain without such agreement.

Second, in the United States, and to some extent also in the Soviet Union, there has been a keen speculative interest in the notion of "firebreaks"—restraints on the conduct of military conflict designed to prevent, or at least impede, escalation from lower to higher levels of violence. They are marked by distinctions, easily recognized, for limiting force.[58] One function attributed to "firebreaks" is that of controlling inadvertent escalation, by giving two nuclear powers suddenly caught in the unplanned eruption of a minor conflict time to ascertain the opponent's intentions, to come to their senses, and to terminate the conflict before it moves up the escalation ladder. Another function sometimes attributed to "firebreaks" is that of permitting the conduct of low-level, and presumably localized, conflict without an unacceptable risk of escalation to a level of warfare which it is in the interest of both adversaries to avoid.[59] Thus, some experts believe that there is a great difference in escalatory potential between the use of conventional armaments and tactical nuclear weapons, and that escalation of limited conflict could be more easily controlled if the use of any nuclear arms were forgone. Others have argued that, if both nuclear powers have an overwhelming interest in shunning mutual mass destruction, even the employment of non-strategic nuclear weapons, or the nonstrategic use of nuclear weapons, should be safe.

This second function of "firebreaks" would serve the purpose of extending the utility of conventional or non-strategic nuclear armaments in conflicts between nuclear powers, though they would do so by depriving strategic weapons of their ability to deter all kinds of conflicts between such powers. War at a restricted level of violence would become more feasible than it would be if escalation were impossible or very hard to control.

If limited local war is to provide a terminal stage of military conflict between the superpowers, both must

[58] Thomas C. Schelling, *The Strategy of Conflict*, Cambridge: Harvard University Press, 1960, pp. 257ff.
[59] For detailed presentation and analysis of such "firebreaks," see Kahn, *On Escalation*.

necessarily find an outcome more appealing than exposure to more violent levels of conflict. Regarding the threshold marked by the introduction of tactical nuclear arms in a local war, it has indeed been argued forcefully that this firebreak is broad and reliable as long as the governments of both powers are inspired by a stark fear of all-out strategic war, and are afraid that escalation is much more probable once any kind of nuclear arms, especially tactical nuclear weapons, are introduced. The more they fear that escalation may be automatic after the nuclear threshold has been crossed, the more they should be aware of the fact that crossing that threshold means entrusting one's destiny to a possibly reckless opponent. Under these circumstances, it is said, the fear of violating the most critical threshold will induce the superpowers to proceed with utmost restraint, and make them most reluctant to escalate a local engagement conducted with non-nuclear arms.[60] In the United States, under the administration of President Kennedy, this set of arguments led to a considerable build-up of conventional forces, based on the so-called doctrine of flexible response. According to this strategic doctrine, the United States must have military capabilities enabling it to proportion any military response to its particular provocation and not to remain excessively dependent on a threat of nuclear retaliation, for this deterrent threat might confront the country with the awful dilemma, in the event that a crisis involves important values, of whether to escalate to the holocaust of mutual annihilation or to give in to the adversary's pressure and ruthlessness. Such an "impossible choice" would almost surely produce a "paralysis of decision."[61]

[60] Cf. Otto Heilbrunn, *Conventional War in the Nuclear Age*, New York: Praeger, 1965, pp. 17ff.
[61] *Ibid.*, chap. 1.

Several arguments can be raised against this line of reasoning. It may well be true that military escalation can be controlled as long as the application of force remains highly localized and adheres to an exceedingly low level of violence. This happened during the Cuban missiles crisis, which was satisfactorily resolved, although under the shadow of strategic nuclear capabilities. In this instance, progressive escalation was not at all automatic; there proved to be "down escalators" as well as "up escalators."[62] On such a relatively low level of conflict, the communication of resolve or despair may restrain an opponent from proceeding to a more serious provocation, and thus in effect prevent war. Yet it is hard to see that escalation would be as easy to control if troops of the two superpowers were engaged in considerable and prolonged combat with one another, if casualties had occurred, and if—as would be likely—the original stakes of conflict had become inflated by the very fact that a military engagement was taking place. Several factors might push one or the other government to make the conflagration leap across the firebreak. A belligerent enjoying superiority on the conventional level might be tempted to press his advantage and raise the price of settlement in various ways. Contrariwise, a belligerent doing poorly in limited conflict might be tempted to improve his position by escalating to a degree. In fact, even if the governments involved were prepared to keep cool heads in a situation fraught with enormous dangers, the public in either nation—unless it were fully aware of the risks being run—might become aroused to righteous indignation and urge its government to abandon restraint. And escalation to the employment of tactical nuclear weapons might occur be-

[62] See the analysis of Albert and Roberta Wohlstetter, *Controlling the Risks in Cuba*, Adelphi Papers (London), No. 17 (April 1965), pp. 18f.

cause of a failure of command and control in a tense situation, or because one antagonist or both, thinking escalation imminent or unavoidable sooner or later, decided to pre-empt; and unlike present conditions on the strategic level, the advantage of striking first in a tactical situation might be considerable and attractive.

Another question may be posed. If escalation can be controlled because the interest of both antagonists to avoid large-scale strategic war is overwhelming, why should not all rungs on the escalation ladder, short of this extreme level of violence, keep conflict limited? Why should the restriction of hostilities to non-nuclear weapons be the crucial threshold? Why would a hard-pressed power not bring tactical nuclear arms into play, although perhaps with a defensive mode of employment? No matter which lower level of conflict were reached, one might speculate, the great-power belligerents would do their utmost to prevent the final step up the escalation ladder. Perhaps even limited strategic war might then be possible without escalation to the cataclysmic level.[63]

But this line of speculation also suggests that the lower-level thresholds are not very high. It can therefore be argued that the emphasis on limited war on a low level, and especially on the "conventional option," has the grave disadvantage of encouraging the aggressive initiation of such conflicts. As has been argued, this is not in the interest of nuclear great powers, for any proposed preference for limiting war to a conventional contest tends to degrade the deterrent value of their nuclear stockpiles.[64] The United States, for example, might find it far harder, with such a policy, to cope with massive Chinese ag-

[63] Cf. Klaus Knorr and Thornton Read (eds.), Limited Strategic War, New York: Praeger, 1962, esp. chaps. 1, 2, 3, 8.
[64] Cf. Bernard Brodie, "What Price Conventional Capabilities in Europe?" The Reporter, May 23, 1963, pp. 25-29.

gression in Asia.[65] As we pointed out above, this is indeed a fair criticism. To increase the feasibility of limited war is to deprive, under the balance of mutual terror, strategic capabilities of their power to deter all but the mildest applications of military force against a nuclear great power. And there is a further implication to be pondered. Whichever school of thought is more realistic, it can scarcely be denied that any military conflict between nuclear powers has *some* probability of escalating —abruptly or gradually—to the large-scale strategic level, if only as a result of inadvertence. We do not wish to exaggerate this possibility, for knowledgeable leaders everywhere might well hesitate to the point of paralysis before doing anything likely to touch off a catastrophic train of events. But it cannot be taken for granted that they will succeed in averting disaster. However small, the possibility cannot be ignored. If this is conceded, then it is possible that a policy of firebreaks that encourages the initiation of limited military conflicts, or discourages them less than would be the case otherwise, may actually increase the probability of the nuclear holocaust more than a policy that keeps the danger of escalation high and thus gives the powers the strongest incentive to shun all military conflict, at least as long as the balance of terror obtains.

Since nuclear powers have hitherto avoided direct military clashes, and we lack pertinent experience, the speculations discussed above are wholly hypothetical. So much turns on the subjective perceptions of the key actors, and these are practically impossible to predict. We have no way of knowing whether, in the event of a direct military confrontation between nuclear powers, the maintenance of firebreaks would be feasible and, if so,

[65] Bernard Brodie, "The McNamara Phenomenon," *World Politics*, xvii (July 1965), p. 682.

where they would be located on the spectrum of increasing violence. It seems plausible to assume that the chances for viable firebreaks would be increased if nuclear powers firmly embedded this concept in their military doctrine and war plans, if they adjusted their military capabilities accordingly, and if—in one way or another—they let each other know that they had done so. There is no conclusive evidence that this has happened.

Soviet strategic thinking, as expressed in public, has until recently derided any idea of keeping a war between the nuclear superpowers restricted. This expression of Soviet doctrine may have been intended to serve the deterrent posture of the Soviet Union—that is, have constituted a part of its declaratory policy—and may not therefore have reflected actual Soviet thinking on the subject. It is also true that Soviet writings have expressed more recently some grudging interest in the possibility of limited local—and even entirely conventional—war in Europe and, more so, outside Europe. Yet the dominant Soviet emphasis is still on the risk that small conflicts will rapidly expand into general war; and that, once tactical nuclear weapons are brought into action, it is infeasible to distinguish between tactical and strategic targets.[66]

One is led to suspect, in conclusion, that escalation from limited conflict between nuclear powers should not be assumed to be automatic. The interests in halting it are, at present at least, very solid indeed. On the other hand, the uncertainty about whether escalation can be avoided looms very large. And this uncertainty itself is therefore apt to deter these powers from lightly initiating even the most limited application of military force against

[66] Thomas W. Wolfe, *Trends in Soviet Thinking on Theater Warfare, Conventional Preparations, and Limited War*, RAND Corp., Memorandum RM-4505-PR. pp. 41ff.

each other. This means that, given the reigning balance of terror, a structure of strategic capabilities that, in Herman Kahn's nomenclature,[67] should afford only "Type I Deterrence" affords also a considerable degree of "Type II Deterrence"—the ability to deter escalation to nuclear war from lesser and local clashes.

Another qualification that we must now introduce turns on our assumptions regarding an existing mutual balance of terror and the consequences of this balance. These assumptions must now be questioned. To begin with, the foregoing analysis treated the two nuclear powers as if they were interchangeable—that is, as if both were equally determined to avoid large-scale nuclear war. This may, in fact, be the case, at least at this juncture. Even if it is, however, it does not follow that they are of necessity equally eager to avoid or minimize the risk of such a war. Usually, the value at stake in a conflict, and other factors such as the personalities of the decision-makers, also bear on behavior under the restraint of risk. It may be assumed, of course, that such differences are likely to be of negligible or no consequence when the risk involves the disaster of nuclear war. Yet this might not be true, especially if there is an expectation that some sort of firebreak will operate in a limited conflict and greatly minimize the risk. To be sure, in such conflict each opponent would face not only the other's limited-war forces, but also *some* risk of uncontrolled escalation. But this suggests that the risk is capable of different estimation. Moreover, these conflicts would be contests of will in which opponents may attempt to manipulate the risk to their advantage. They may have a strong incentive to do so if their stake is of high value, and particularly if it seems to them more valuable than what is at stake for the

[67] Kahn, *On Thermonuclear War*, pp. 126-44.

other antagonist. A balance of motivation, or of resolution, thus becomes part of the effective balance of
bargaining strength. There is, furthermore, also a very
important skill element in the reciprocal manipulation of
risk. The skill of rightly estimating the opponent's nerve
and control in the course of a tense crisis may permit
bargaining exploitation of what one expert has called
"the narrow margin of freedom of action that eludes
nuclear deterrence."[68] Perhaps not too much should be
made of these possibilities, but they should not be ruled
out.

What if we drop the assumption of a stable mutual
balance of terror, based, as it must be, on the assured and
known second-strike capability of each nuclear power
to cause disastrous damage to the other's cities and
population? If only one of two nuclear powers possessed
this capability, it would enjoy significant military superiority over the other, and could exploit its position in
order to press the other to make concessions about
foreign-policy issues. Subject to restraints to be noted
later, the superior power could then derive a great deal
of utility from its strategic and limited-war capabilities—
not perhaps from brazenly initiating or threatening war
but from its lesser fear of war in the course of a diplomatic crisis; and should limited hostilities break out, it
would clearly enjoy "escalation dominance." Even if the
known balance of nuclear forces were such as to produce
serious doubts about whether a truly mutual balance of
terror prevailed, or whether one power was strategically
superior to the other, the beneficiary of the doubt would
be in a position to press harder than its opponent for a
satisfactory settlement of disputes.

[68] Général André Beaufré, *Introduction à la stratégie*, Paris:
Armand Colin, 1963, p. 98.

INSTABILITIES IN THE BALANCE OF TERROR

The widespread conviction that the balance of terror now believed to exist between the Soviet Union and the United States will endure for a long time to come, and thus constitute a fixed datum, has been endorsed in recent years with amazing certitude. Not only has the short history of nuclear competition between the two powers been marked by remarkable ups and downs in their relative capabilities, with the United States enjoying a significant degree of superiority much of the time; this history has also revealed serious limitations to estimating and comparing the true military relationship between the two strategic capabilities without a considerable time lag. The widespread belief, in the late 1950's and in 1960, in the existence of a "missile gap" greatly favoring the USSR—a belief that was subsequently proven erroneous —is a case in point. How, then, can one be sure that the balance of terror, assuming it to hold at present, will endure in the future?

Current belief in a balance of terror is based on the assumption that each of the powers possesses an unquestionable offensive capacity to obliterate the other, even if one launches a first strike against the other's means of nuclear reprisal, and that technology is unable to come up with active defenses against nuclear missiles efficient enough to rob the offense of its present decisive superiority. To be sure, anti-ballistic-missile (ABM) defenses have been developed, but it has been generally assumed, at least until very recently, that if one opponent deployed such defenses, the other could always saturate them if he produced—at an expense falling far short of the expense of ABM's—more missiles and a variety of penetration aids such as decoys on which ABM forces would waste the short precious time available for action against incoming missiles.

It is entirely possible, and perhaps probable, that neither the Soviet Union nor the United States will develop and deploy large-scale and near-perfect defenses. Perhaps the development of an improved ABM technology will fail to touch off a new phase in the arms race between the nuclear superpowers—a race between the means of penetration and the means of interception, between the forces for assuring the destruction of the opponent and those designed to limit the damage he can inflict. And even if both sides deploy substantial defensive capabilities, the outcome may well be that neither side will develop confidence in its ability to fend off the other's attack. But even under these assumptions, the balance of terror might be seriously affected and look more fragile than it does at the present time. Of course, the balance would gain in stability if ABM's were deployed only for protecting the retaliatory forces, thus rendering them less vulnerable than they might be otherwise, and adding assurance to each antagonist's ability to devastate the other. Yet if they were installed to afford substantial protection to populations, then they would—even were they far from perfect—introduce new uncertainties, and thus tend to destabilize the condition of nuclear terror; and this particularly if only one side proceeded to large-scale deployment.

Modern science and technology, however, are too dynamic to make one sure that ABM's will not be developed with an efficiency capable of seriously undermining, if not ending completely, the present superiority of the offense.[69] What if technology comes up with a

[69] For an argument showing that technological change may not, and is perhaps unlikely to, upset the currently stable balance of deterrence, see Arnold M. Kuzmack, "Technological Change and

"splendid defense"? Of course, if for a time only one side developed and installed effective defenses, it would gain a decisive strategic superiority, completely upsetting the balance of terror. Yet this is very unlikely to happen, since both sides are devoting considerable resources to relevant research and development, and since the large-scale deployment of ABM systems would probably be a gradual process, and one that could hardly be concealed from a watchful opponent. Still, a degree of temporary advantage might result. This advantage would probably not be great enough to preclude the other power's ability to deter a direct attack on itself; but it might make it attractive to the advantaged power to engineer serious crises, possibly including limited military conflict, and exact a high price for their settlement. In brief, the power with ABM success might be far less deterred than the other from initiating courses of action now considered too risky. By diminishing the opponent's confidence in his offensive power, superior defensive capabilities would encourage an aggressive posture.

Should both powers develop and deploy very good though not splendid ABM systems, mutual nuclear deterrence would certainly become more complicated than it is at present. The vulnerability of both populations, and hence their role as hostages to the good behavior of their governments, would be more or less diminished, and so would the power to deter. Even if neither side had an incentive to attack the other directly, the risks that lesser provocations might escalate to the intolerable round of destruction would be seriously impaired. Stability at the strategic level—an appreciably different stability from the present one—would be accompanied by

Stable Deterrence," *Journal of Conflict Resolution*, IX (September 1965), pp. 309-17.

greater instability at lower levels of international violence. In fact, the political utility of military power might be extended considerably beyond its present narrow scope.

As already acknowledged, none of this may happen. Large-scale ABM systems may not be installed, or parallel advances in offensive capabilities may checkmate the new defenses. It cannot be taken for granted, however, that it will not happen. Viewed in retrospect, the balance of terror may never have been "delicate," especially when intangibles are taken into account. But it is "to complex and too changeable" to warrant belief in its permanence.[70] This is so for several reasons. It may be upset by the development of new technology, perhaps because one power possesses better research and development resources than the other, or administers them to better effect, or is lucky in invention, or owns more skill in innovation[71]—that is, in the military exploitation of evolving technological choices. With technological invention and innovation being rather unpredictable, as they notably were during the past twenty-five years, important differences between the two powers might—for this and other reasons—develop in force structures and magnitudes, in military doctrine and in facilities for command and control; and such differences might make the balance of terror less "mutual." Differences in the information which each side possesses about the other's capabilities and plans might, from time to time, generate significant asymmetries in their ability to deter. Finally, there are various political and psychological factors that condition deterrent power, all subject over time to change that

[70] Wohlstetter, *Controlling the Risks in Cuba*, p. 24.

[71] On the difference between military invention and innovation, and their conditions, see Klaus Knorr and Oskar Morgenstern, *Science and Defense*, Center of International Studies, Princeton University, Policy Memorandum No. 32, 1965.

may prove destabilizing in the overall balance rather than compensatory. Leaders will change and may differ in skill, in their ability to keep cool under the stresses of crisis, in their disposition to run risks and to gamble, and in the political pressures to which they are subjected, especially in crises, by rivals for leadership, by larger publics, and by allies. The values at stake in conflict are highly variable. In other words, there is no such thing —as is too often assumed—as an absolute ability to deter, fixed in power and constant at all times regardless of changeable circumstances. Rather, the power to deter is the power to deter a particular adversary in a particular situation. These particulars are apt to change over time; and deterrence cannot be insensitive to all these changes.

Uncertainties even about the present balance of terror, dissatisfaction with the present restricted utility of military power, and uncertainties about whether the strategic balance will remain stable give the governments of both superpowers an incentive to continue the quantitative, and especially the qualitative, arms race, and thus to set in motion forces capable of upsetting the present conditions of stability. Given various uncertainties, a margin of military superiority looks desirable. The incentive to escape from their present position of being locked in a stalemate of strategic threat and counterthreat—provided there are means of escape that are technologically, economically, politically, and perhaps morally feasible—is reinforced by the desire to reduce damage in the event of inadvertent war and to counter any threat from new nuclear powers that are incapable of mounting an attack with which even ABM's of presently available properties cannot cope. Nor is the problem only one of efficient ABM's. More advanced and "exotic" weapons systems may issue from the laboratories.

It is true that the arms race is expensive and its outcome uncertain. Each side must fear that it might confer a degree of temporary advantage on the other. For each the future might be worse than the present; larger defense efforts might lead to lesser security. In terms of long-run security, therefore, both governments might recognize an interest in preserving present conditions and hence in calling off or slackening the race. The trouble is that this shared interest can be satisfied only if the suspension of the arms race is jointly organized, formally or informally. Unfortunately, the suspension of the qualitative arms race, of the pursuit of military research and development, is practically impossible to verify. Given the profusion of laboratories in each country, the evasion of an agreement, whether formal or tacit, is relatively easy; and if only for protection against the other's possible evasion, the inducement to evade is considerable. Under these circumstances, it requires a good deal of optimism to believe that the great powers will do anything else but pursue courses of action likely to undermine the degree of stability now extant. They might refrain from deploying new systems by mutual understanding; they are less likely to refrain from pressing their development; and if they believe a developed system spells a more than marginal improvement in their military capabilities, the temptation to deploy would be strong, and perhaps irresistible.

To conclude, the leaders of the two superpowers cannot know now what the opponent's force structure will be five or ten years hence. Existing known types of arms may be vastly improved, and entirely novel weapons may show up in the armories. A host of relevant political conditions may change. It is fair to ask: What does "mutuality" of deterrence mean as one tries to look into the future? Perhaps the best available basis for a lasting balance of terror will be that—although many factors in the present strategic equation change—their implication will be highly uncertain, singly and especially in combination. Utter lack of confidence in what would happen if *the* "button," or any one of a series of buttons, were pushed might for some time to come preserve the present degree of stability between the nuclear great powers.

THE RESTRICTED USABILITY OF MILITARY FORCES

Unquestionably, the conditions, and especially the costs, of using force as an instrument of foreign policy have undergone a major permutation in the nuclear age. As between the two nuclear great powers locked in a balance of terror, military power is actively usable for a far smaller range of political purposes than was the case between great powers before the nuclear era. The very behavior of the two powers toward one another can be regarded as evidence to this effect. Even though tension between them has been high, and conflicts often sharp, they have treated each other with great circumspection in the military area; and this caution is generally credited to their eagerness to avoid general war. Indeed, this caution makes them shun any direct military confrontation. They prefer war by proxy to war between themselves. They prefer vague threats to specific threats of war. They do not seem eager to have diplomatic disputes escalate into intense crises. Hitherto their fear of monstrous destruction seems to have made them unwilling to use force or the threat of force bluntly as a sanction in diplomatic bargaining; and the movement toward a *détente* in Soviet-American relations that set in after the Cuban missiles crisis can be interpreted as manifesting a mutual desire to avoid dangerous crises.

This behavior, of course, expresses a profound appreciation of military force. Deterrence of provocative behavior rests on such appreciation. But, as we have seen, there is more to it than that. Within this tightly restrained situation, these powers tend to use their military strength on behalf of foreign-policy objectives in a subtle and highly controlled manner. The risk of escalation may be very dangerous to both; yet, if foreign-policy stakes are sufficiently high, they do not refrain from manipulating this risk to their advantage. In each past crisis, both faced the risk that a direct military confrontation might occur, and if it did, the further risk that a limited conflict would escalate. This presence of deadly risk makes each crisis a dangerous test of wills—a test in which the threat of military force is likely to be used only in a most discreet fashion, as, for example, in the course of several crises over Berlin and the crisis over the Cuban missiles. As has been observed by others, in pursuing their foreign policies and in arriving at crisis settlements, the great nuclear powers do not use nuclear war, but exploit the fear of it.[72] They exploit the risk of war rather than relative military power; they negotiate less from strength than from relative susceptibility to fear and worry.[73]

In order to understand this introduction of military power by the great powers in crisis management, we must look at the components of crisis behavior. A crisis between great powers is an unstable sequence of inter-actions, of tacit or explicit bargaining moves, at an intense level of confrontation that increases the probability of international violence. Nevertheless, one must not exaggerate the function of military power in crisis situations, important as it is. The personality of leaders, the freedom of action they have in terms of national politics

[72] Robert Dickson Carr, "A New Cold War?" *Survival,* VII (March-April 1965), pp. 79ff.

[73] Coral Bell, *Negotiation from Strength,* New York: Knopf, 1963, chap. 7.

and commitment to alliances, and the skill of governments are also important determinants of the outcome of crises, of whether they end in peaceful adjustment, or unresolved deadlock, or cause the eruption of military hostilities. The personality of leaders is important in affecting their ability to stand up under pressures, including the pressures resulting from anxiety and the speed with which events take place. Leaders also differ in rationality, the degree to which they are subject to emotion in making decisions, in their propensity to gamble and act with daring in managing a severe crisis, and so on. The freedom of action that leaders enjoy affects the range of feasible options open to them. The skill of leaders is important in how they cope with domestic pressure and the entreaties of allies; and it is crucial in managing the intergovernmental bargaining process with the adversary. This management may involve attempts to alter the opponent's perception of the situation by giving him information about one's arms, capabilities, and resolve. It involves the holding out of rewards since no crises, and especially no crisis proceeding under the shadow of nuclear capabilities, is lacking in common interests, and hence, in the language of game theory, is not merely a "zero-sum game"; it has a cooperative as well as a competitive aspect.[74] The derivation of influence from the promise of reward may take such forms as the offer of acceptable concessions to the opponent's demands and the offer of a line of retreat from excessive demands that enables him to save face before his domestic and the international public. And skill is obviously crucial in the manipulation of threats, tacit or explicit, of impending military action. The trading of threats and counterthreats goes to the heart of the test of wills; and it is the manipulation of military threats between great nuclear powers that has become so dangerous because

[74] Cf. Schelling, *The Strategy of Conflict*, esp. chap. 4.

of the looming disaster of all-out nuclear war, and the risk that lesser military confrontations may escalate to this level. As long as a balance of terror prevails between the opponents, and the temptation of a pre-emptive strike by surprise is accordingly small, there is less pressure to make fateful decisions without deliberation; and there is also hope that abrupt moves up the escalation ladder can be avoided even if a rather limited application of force takes place. Nevertheless, the trading of military threats is much more risky when the opponents are nuclear powers than usually was the case before the nuclear age. The willingness to assume the risk and, by increasing it for the opponent, also to increase it for one-self depends on the factors already mentioned (e.g., the personalities of the leaders, their freedom of action) and, in addition, on the relation of military strength, as perceived by each opponent, and on the stakes for each involved in the crisis. Thus, the risks are, or appear to be, unequal because one antagonist has, or believes he has, a significant degree of military superiority; and the issue at stake may be of much greater value to one actor than to the other. One may minimize risk by assuming bargaining positions that leave acceptable options of retreat, that balance ends and means at the least danger-ous level of crisis interaction; one may raise risks by as-suming positions from which one cannot extricate oneself without large disadvantages in terms of loss of face, political influence, self-respect, etc.—that is, by deliber-ately making commitments from which it is extremely hard to be relieved. The mutual manipulation of military threats is apt to lead to change in the actor's perceptions as the crisis proceeds, and produces a kind of quick learn-ing process through which risks and resolve are reevalu-ated. Mao points out that "war is a contest of strength," but that "the original state of strength changes in the course of war."[75] So it is with severe crises. They are a contest of wills, but the initial relation of their strengths is apt to change, and perhaps fluctuate, in the course of the crisis. When war can be a massive disaster to both contestants, there is the temptation to paralyze the opponent by threatening this disaster; but the trading of such monstrous threats may end in one's own paralysis.[76] Threat manipulation is so dangerous a game because so much can go wrong in the trading of risks. Under the pressure of time and anxiety, errors may be made, decision-making may become stereotyped rather than flexible and adaptive, more emotional and less rational, and information may be hard to communicate and to receive. In part, the opponent's intentions are seldom known and easily misunderstood. Even if he tries to communicate his real intentions, his message may be suspect, and his intentions are subject to change, and indeed rapid change, in a fast-moving crisis.

Under these circumstances, it is not hard to see why the governments of the two superpowers tread with care, and rarely make explicit threats of violence when in the throes of a crisis; and why—were they ever involved in a direct but low-level military clash—they might understand that "underretaliation" is preferable to "overretaliation."[77] The fear of escalation tends to be inhibiting. In the course of the Cuban missiles crisis, certainly, the specific threat of force was very low-level, although "threats of higher levels of violence were implicit at every stage in the developing crisis,"[78] and were no doubt effective. Where the stakes are high, as in Europe—and,

[75] Mao Tse-tung, *On the Protracted War*, Peking: Foreign Languages Press, 1954, p. 87.
[76] Wohlstetter, *Controlling the Risks in Cuba*, p. 20.
[77] Cf. Deutsch, *The Nerves of Government*, p. 194.
[78] Wohlstetter, *Controlling the Risks in Cuba*, p. 22.

as in the Caribbean, anywhere close to the territories of the two great powers—a direct military confrontation between the two antagonists appears at this time so dangerous that it is virtually inconceivable, except by inadvertence. Even over South Vietnam, in 1965, when the United States greatly increased its commitment, including the commitment of its prestige, the Soviet Union as well as China behaved with extreme caution. As a British commentator put it, the conflict in Vietnam "appeared to have reduced the international scene to a state of frozen immobility."[79] Even a small risk of precipitating nuclear war obviously serves to inhibit the use of military power; its most valuable payoff is the payoff of the threat rather than its execution, and of the implicit rather than of the explicit threat. Nevertheless, military power has been used in a fashion—over Berlin, over Cuba, and over South Vietnam. Even under conditions of nuclear parity, and the competitive manipulation of a deadly risk, strategic nuclear power is of instrumental value, and thus of some political utility.

There is indeed a weighty factor running counter to the posture of caution assumed by the Soviet Union and the United States. This factor is inherent in the role of protector which the two great powers have taken on. Not only do both have numerous allies, but there are also other states whose policy toward one great power is partially governed by the expectation its government has of receiving support in a pinch from the other great power. The so-called "domino theory," at times espoused in the United States, expresses an awareness of this circumstance. According to this doctrine, Thailand will fall under Communist control if South Vietnam does, Burma will if Thailand does, and so on. In its crude form, the

[79] *Manchester Guardian Weekly*, July 15, 1965, p. 1.

domino theory may serve to distort reality more than to illuminate it, for the behavior of the "domino" states is not simply a product of the condition singled out by this view. Yet the value of Soviet and United States protection tends to fluctuate delicately with a vast range of behavior taken as indicative of their ability and willingness to intervene on behalf of a nation pressed by the other great power or one of its allies. Changes in military capabilities, deployment, and expenditures, and in the content and tone of official and unofficial announcements, are watched and interpreted from this point of view by the interested parties. The pattern of behavior in international crises is indubitably regarded as the most telling indicator of "protective worth." Thus, the value of the United States as a protector tends to go down if this country is deemed to act with timidity in a crisis over Berlin or Laos, and it tends to go up if it acts with forthright vigor in South Vietnam or the Caribbean. It is not rare, when the United States acts with especial military aplomb and pugnacity, as it did in Lebanon in 1958, for a foreign critic to berate the United States on political or moral grounds while simultaneously deriving assurance from the display of the American willingness to act boldly. The United States and the Soviet Union are thus sometimes placed in the difficult position of having to decide whether or not the penalties of non-involvement in a crisis exceed the advantages.

But in direct confrontations, it is in subtle, indirect, and severely restrained ways that military power is exerted between the nuclear states. The importance of this fact cannot be overstressed. But, though this amounts to an important qualification of our first conclusion, that conclusion is by no means dissipated. When risks are suicidal, or close to suicidal, war and the threat of war are shunned and compromise more readily accepted.

Past behavior exhibits the painstaking care the two superpowers take in avoiding a direct military confrontation even of a highly localized and limited sort. When one of them intervenes abroad militarily, the other will rigorously castigate such action but refrain from military counterinvention. Thus, the United States stood by when the Soviet Union crushed the Hungarian uprising; and the Soviet Union remained on the sidelines when the United States directly intervened in the South Vietnamese civil war. It is interesting to note the very gradual way, carefully circumscribed in each stage, in which the United States stepped up its military intervention in 1965, including the limited bombardment of North Vietnam. The highly controlled escalation in which the United States engaged was probably dictated by several prudential considerations. One may speculate that a regard for world public opinion, including American public opinion, was a consideration, and that another was the aim not to put the Soviet Union at any one time under too much pressure to resort to a form of intervention that would be risky for both superpowers. Nevertheless, the Kremlin probably felt and yet resisted considerable pressure, made especially acute by Peking's accusations, to come effectively to the aid of Communist North Vietnam. Both powers were pulling their military punches. Using military power more boldly would have meant exposure to mortal danger.

CHAPTER V

THE OTHER POWERS:

NUCLEAR AND NON-NUCLEAR

T HE PLACE AND functions of military power in the international affairs of the nuclear age must now be examined beyond the confrontation of the two superpowers, although this confrontation, necessarily and importantly, impinges on all other uses of military force by the nuclear great powers themselves and by other states.

SUPERPOWERS VERSUS OTHER NUCLEAR POWERS

If there are severe restraints on the usability of military force between the superpowers in one respect, this usability is for them greater in their relations with lesser nuclear powers. However, even though in any such encounter the superpower need not fear enormous damage to itself, the usefulness of bringing its military superiority into play is restricted considerably. It is, of course, reduced by the diminished legitimacy of war and hence by the costs which illegitimate applications of force may generate. It is also restricted by the special stigma attached to the employment of nuclear bombs—a subject further discussed below. It is limited by the support which the superpower may lend to the lesser nuclear state facing another nuclear superpower. And it is, finally, restricted by whatever retaliation the smaller power may threaten to wreak on the greater nuclear power. This last restraint, the ability to deter, is sensitive to the differences in strategic capabilities, particularly in the ability of nuclear strike forces to penetrate defenses and destroy their targets and, very important, in the difference in the vulnerability of these forces to a pre-emptive attack. These disparities can obviously be very great, even between such powers as the Soviet Union and Great Britain, or the United States and Communist China. Vulnerability of the lesser powers to a disarming or blunting attack may decrease to the extent they are able, technologically and economically, to afford the survival-increasing means of dispersion, mobility, concealment, hardening, and multiplication of nuclear retaliatory systems. But unless numbers increase greatly and sophisticated penetration aids are available—in which case the lesser power would, in terms of nuclear capability, approach the rank of the superpowers—the problem of penetration may be crucial. This would be especially true if, as discussed in Chapter IV, each superpower proceeds to deploy ABM defenses that, though perhaps inadequate to deal with a saturation attack by the other superpower, may be capable of countering the small-scale or ragged attack a lesser nuclear power is able to mount. That is to say, its capacity to inflict severe punishment on great nuclear powers may be very limited, dubious, or flatly lacking. With the intensity of mutual threats being very, and perhaps grossly, unequal, it is also likely that the credibility of the threats will be unequal, and so then is deterrent power. It would surely be rash to conclude that military superiority is a meaningless concept when great nuclear powers are pitted against the small. The latter's fear of retaliation should be paramount.

It follows that in the risk-trading of an international crisis between nuclear powers whose capabilities are known to be substantially unequal, the government of the lesser power runs a comparatively far greater, and ulti-

mately deadly, risk, and this should give the great power
the easy upper hand. Even if, in such a confrontation of
unequals, the great nuclear power is self-deterred for
one reason or another from using its nuclear might, or
from making explicit nuclear threats, the implicit threat
is there and its government can press much harder for a
settlement on its terms; and if limited war occurred, it
would probably enjoy escalation dominance. Thus, decidedly lesser nuclear powers cannot afford to pursue
toward a superior nuclear power a high-risk policy involving a high level of international violence. Nuclear
powers equipped, in Leo Szilard's phrase, only with "the
sting of the bee"[80]—the bee that dies after he has stung—
are unlikely to inspire as much terror as they themselves
experience; and this lack of real mutuality may give the
military capabilities of the superior powers utility of a
wider range.

However, nuclear powers of distinctly lesser than
first rank may command the power to deter other nations
with roughly equal or lesser capabilities. Our analysis of
the relationship between the superpowers should apply
to these relations—except, of course, that these relations
exist in the presence of superior nuclear powers which
might intervene in one form or another, and this fact
might complicate the "balance of terror" among nations
on the inferior levels.

NUCLEAR PROLIFERATION

At present there are five nuclear powers, although at
least one, China, was in 1965 and 1966 only nominally so.
It is extremely probable that more national nuclear
powers will appear on the scene during the next ten or
twenty years. Following its pioneering phase, the tech-

[80] Leo Szilard, "The Sting of the Bee in 'Saturation Parity,' "
Bulletin of the Atomic Scientists, March 1965, pp. 8ff.

nology of manufacturing nuclear bombs is becoming simpler and cheaper, and the relevant technological knowledge has become widely diffused. Scientific education and engineering training are progressing everywhere, and programs for the peaceful exploitation of atomic energy spread familiarity with nuclear processes and their control, and make plutonium available to many countries in increasing quantities. Aircraft for simple delivery can be readily procured by most nations, the technology of building rockets is becoming more widely known, and rockets of modest lift and range are becoming commercially available for importation. It is getting easier to become a nuclear power of sorts.

Among nations currently credited with the ability to develop nuclear weapons are Sweden, Switzerland, the Federal Republic of Germany, Canada, Israel, Italy, India, Japan, and Australia. The incentives and disincentives acting on governments pondering whether or not to "go nuclear" are complex and vary necessarily from country to country. There are weighty disincentives of obvious economic and moral concern. To these must be added a political inconvenience for nations that have for many years denounced the wickedness of nuclear weaponry and clamored for nuclear disarmament; and there are even military disadvantages to be specified below. Finally, there is the special drawback that nearly all nations are party to the agreement prohibiting nuclear testing in the atmosphere, although the treaty makes provision for withdrawal upon three months' notice. Arrayed against these negative considerations are beliefs, even if ambivalent, in the military utility of nuclear arms; dubious claims that the development of military nuclear systems is favorable, if not indispensable, to modern industrial development; and cravings for nuclear armament as a symbol of international status and, within nations, as a source of prestige for governments, scientists, and the military. It will presumably be concrete problems of this kind peculiar to the national and international situation of particular countries that will tip the balance in most instances. An India made to feel insecure by the posture of China, or an Israel pressed by hostile Arab states, may decide to go ahead; and if they do, their neighbors will feel constrained to consider or reconsider their position in the local balance of military power. Indeed, it would be a mistake to underrate the incentives that will push countries along the nuclear route, especially since a very modest nuclear capability may serve to justify the hankering after prestige, and have some defensive and deterrent value against similarly equipped neighbors; while the development of such a nuclear presence may happen step by step, no single one looking too expensive, or requiring serious consideration of the next one.

Both nuclear superpowers, as well as many other nations, have voiced a strong interest in impeding the proliferation of national nuclear capabilities. Their governments are convinced that proliferation will tend to make the world a more dangerous place for all nations; and it may also be presumed that they sense proliferation as a development apt to lessen their own military power and prestige. However, exhortation apart, the means available to the superpowers for pursuing an anti-proliferation policy are all too costly to them in one way or another. They could extend "nuclear guarantees," that is, offer non-nuclear countries protection from nuclear attack or blackmail by other nuclear powers; they could employ power to force prospective candidates to desist; they could have recourse to the threat of various diplomatic and economic reprisals in order to obstruct or at least slow down proliferation; and they could strengthen their moral position, as well as the disincentives of possible candidates for nuclear stature, by forswearing the use of nuclear weapons and by proceeding forthwith to at least partial nuclear disarmament. The trouble with all these policies is that they entail various disadvantages, and though these costs could be greatly reduced, this could be achieved only if the superpowers acted in complete concert. There is no sign that they are seriously prepared to do so at the present time.

Assuming that a degree of nuclear proliferation will occur in the future, we may also assume that national nuclear capabilities will vary markedly in their military capacity and value. Three classes of nuclear powers might be distinguished. First, there are the great nuclear powers with huge investments in their military forces, capable both of enormous reinvestments and of remaining in the vanguard of advancing military technology. For some time to come, this rank will be occupied only by the two superpowers now in existence. A united Europe, were it to unite, and perhaps a determined Japan, could aspire to the same status after efforts requiring a considerable number of years to bring it to fruition; and possibly China could manage the ascent in a more distant future. Second, there would be nuclear middle powers, such as the United Kingdom and France at present. This is a rank accessible to all modern industrial countries, and to China after some years or a decade of development. The third category will be represented by nations unable, unless assisted by more resourceful countries, to manage more than a small capability consisting of technologically primitive nuclear bombs and delivery systems.

We have already indicated the utility which Class A powers are likely to derive from their nuclear capabilities in relations with one another; in general, similar utilities should accrue to members of each lower class with reference to other powers of roughly equal dimension. More significant might be the utilities available to members of the first two classes in relations with nations of inferior nuclear capabilities—utilities arising from their superior power to deter armed attack and other aggressive behavior, and also from their ability to subject powers of lesser rank to pressures on behalf of various demands. The realization of these advantages would be conditioned, however—perhaps heavily so—by cross-rank alliances and by the threat of intervention on the part of the superpowers. On the other hand, and this is the other side of the coin, all nuclear powers—and notably the great and middle powers—would face an increased risk, inherent in international conflict entanglements, of being caught in nuclear conflict as a result of policies pursued by allies and other states. The flat disutility of becoming involved in nuclear war by inadvertence would hover ominously over all nuclear powers, and especially over those occupying the Class A and B ranks.

NUCLEAR POWERS VERSUS NON-NUCLEAR POWERS

At first sight, nuclear powers should enjoy an unquestionable and valuable military advantage over non-nuclear states and thus be able to derive substantial political benefits from their superiority in military technology. However, several complicating factors require this conclusion to be qualified appreciably. Two of the restraints acting on the governments of nuclear powers have been discussed above. One is generated by the diminished legitimacy of war, and the other by the ability of superior military powers to intervene in favor of a non-nuclear country, whether it is an ally or not. In addition, there are the reasons we advanced in explaining the recently acquired ability of small countries to defy the big powers. Finally, we must note an intangible factor of great import.

The fact is that a kind of stigma, similar to that adhering to chemical and bacteriological weapons, has attached itself to nuclear weapons, and especially to their active use. These weapons are widely regarded with a special awe and horror; and this horror would no doubt be transferred to any nation first detonating nuclear bombs on another.* Hiroshima and Nagasaki are still vividly remembered as symbols of a new frightfulness, and since then nuclear bombs have not been dropped in earnest. An expectation has been created that their use is subject to a severe restraint; it is a restraint that may be growing with each year of non-use.

That is not to say, of course, that nuclear weapons will never be employed in the future. None of the restraints we have discussed is absolute in its power. Each simply imposes a cost on the user which he may be willing to assume when in sufficiently desperate straits. And in the past some leaders have thrown off moral restraints very lightly, as when Italy used poison gas against Ethiopia in the 1930's. The temptation to ignore the stigma may indeed be considerable. It is unlikely, of course, that a nuclear power, particularly a great power, will ever want to launch strategic nuclear explosives against the cities of a non-nuclear country, if only because of the anticipation of excessive costs in terms of international reputation and

* It is interesting to note that the UN General Assembly passed a resolution (No. 1653) in 1961 which bans the use of nuclear weapons. Specifically, it is declared that "the use of nuclear and thermo-nuclear weapons is contrary to the spirit, letter and aims of the United Nations . . ." and ". . . contrary to the laws of humanity and . . . a crime against mankind and civilization. . . ." The resolution was adopted by 55 votes to 20, with 26 abstentions. The United States, the United Kingdom, and France voted against the resolution. Their NATO allies either also voted against or abstained. The communist countries voted affirmatively.

national self-respect. The temptation to use tactical nuclear arms is more likely to arise, particularly when a nuclear great power is faced with a massive superiority of conventional forces in an area in which it finds it hard to deploy adequate counterforces, and do so with dispatch, or in which it finds the prospect of a large-scale, protracted, and bloody conventional war extremely unattractive. This kind of temptation might arise, for example, if the United States became involved with Communist China in a defensive conflict on the Asian mainland—as long as China is only a nominal but not an effective nuclear power—and encountered, as in the course of the Korean War, the brunt of numerous Chinese divisions. The advantage then of using tactical nuclear weapons might not only be to offset an inferiority in conventional strength in an area in which it is hard for the modern forces of a distant power to operate. Their employment might also commend itself where quickness of military response is of the essence, and where the introduction of tactical nuclear weapons might permit a prompt settlement of the conflict. With such possibilities in mind, a number of people in the United States have recently been chafing against the restraints on the use of nuclear weapons. They have been wondering why this country should forgo so great a military asset and instead risk the lives of its conventionally equipped soldiers. In their concern, they have even raised doubts about the existence of the stigma or suggested that the restraint is largely or wholly self-imposed. These considerations have aroused interest in evading the stigma by the development of "clean" tactical bombs whose detonation would be virtually free of radioactive fall-out, whose blast effective would be comparable to that of massive applications of TNT, and whose virtue therefore would lie primarily in the economy of delivery, requiring few rather than many aircraft sorties, or few weapons and men rather than many if fired from a gun. However, a nuclear bomb is likely to be regarded as a nuclear bomb no matter how small the fall-out. And the reality of the stigma is hard to deny and ignore. It certainly is not wholly self-imposed and, to the extent that it is, it is presumably no product of fancy but stems from moral compunctions having a deep reality of their own.

To the extent that the stigma causes restraint, it deprives nuclear armament of usability in combat. Yet its usefulness is not nil, and the possession of tactical nuclear weapons does confer a degree of utility on nuclear powers involved in conflict with non-nuclear nations. On the one hand, the costs of defying the stigma are not a fixed constant, but a variable liability. They would presumably be less, and perhaps far less, if the non-nuclear power behaved with evident and shocking aggressiveness. The nuclear power could further manipulate these costs by proceeding to the employment of tactical nuclear arms with caution and restraint, after due warning in the face of clear-cut provocation, initially perhaps only for exemplary effect or in a visibly defensive role; and, if necessary thereafter, under self-imposed limitations regarding numbers, yields, and targets, and especially with great care to avoid or minimize civilian casualties. Nevertheless, the threshold of justification. variable as it may be, is high, and the option to use tactical nuclear armament is likely to be exercised only with great reluctance. The restraint will tend to be less inhibiting when a severe crisis is at hand, and the stakes are vital. On the other hand, the non-nuclear power can never be sure that, if it presses too hard, the option will not be exercised. This uncertainty is bound to affect its willingness to enter a serious military contest with a nuclear power and would hamper it, if such a contest could not be avoided, in the full deployment of its conventional forces, for these would be vulnerable targets should the nuclear opponent cease to refrain from using its nuclear arms. This alone lends appreciable value to the *possession* of nuclear weapons. And what is more, these contingent advantages derived from the possession of nuclear weapons may, in the first place, deter non-nuclear countries from adopting courses of action likely to end in a dangerous military collision with a nuclear power. Subject to these effects, the relation of non-nuclear capabilities will nevertheless gain in importance to the extent that the cumulative bearing of the several restraints makes it difficult for a nuclear power to decide on employing nuclear arms against a non-nuclear opponent.

The stigma attached to nuclear bombs operates no doubt in placing a restraint on *any* first use, even against a nuclear power. But it may operate more forcefully when the opponent is a non-nuclear country. If this is true, then we perceive a particular military disadvantage which a nation may take into account when deliberating the choice of becoming a nuclear power. If a nation chooses the nuclear option, this might well render it more likely that nuclear weapons will be used against it than would be the case if it stayed in the ranks of the non-nuclear states. It is possible, for example, that Communist China increased its military vulnerability to the United States when it exploded its first bomb. If this holds true, then the *great* nuclear powers will see the value of their nuclear capabilities correspondingly appreciate as proliferation proceeds. On the other hand, whatever gains a presently non-nuclear nation expects to secure by deciding to travel the nuclear road, it stands to forfeit the benefits of some of the restraints at present imposed on the great powers in their relationship with smaller and non-nuclear powers. This is not, of course, a consideration applying to all possible candidates for nuclear status. Thus, India will hardly be kept from "going nuclear" by any anxiety over losing China's forbearance. Her government will be more concerned about the contrary advice of the Soviet Union and the United States, both nations from which India hopes to obtain a degree of protection from Chinese aggression.

WAR BETWEEN NON-NUCLEAR POWERS

With the exception of five states, no nations possess nuclear weapons at the present time; even if a degree of "nuclear proliferation" occurs, the majority of countries will remain non-nuclear, at least for a long time to come. What then about the utility of war between non-nuclear nations, and the value to them of military forces for resolving conflicts involving only members of this very large group of countries? These questions are important, even though it is the great powers and the nuclear nations that present the world with the most acute problems of security. The more than 120 states in the non-nuclear class could fight a great many wars, causing widespread destruction to themselves and, besides, creating circumstances that might bring the great and nuclear powers, and thereby the formidable security problems, into play. In the past, it has often been hostilities among the small fry that led to war between great military powers.

Regarding the propensity, since World War II, of the lesser and non-nuclear countries to fight each other, as distinct from engaging in internal war, the record is certainly not one of total abstention, even if we exclude colonial rebellions from consideration. Colonial rebellion apart, these states have been involved in three types of military confrontation. First, there have been fairly prolonged or large-scale military conflicts between India and Pakistan, Indonesia and Malaysia, Taiwan and mainland

China, and Israel and the surrounding Arab states. Each of these conflicts involved a challenge to the very legitimacy of a particular territorial unit: Kashmir, Malaysia, Taiwan, and Israel. Such remaining colonial possessions as the Portuguese dependencies, and Rhodesia and the Union of South Africa, may become objects of military challenge for similar reasons. Second, frequent border clashes have erupted between such states as Ethiopia and Somalia, Algeria and Morocco, Chile and Argentina, Cambodia and Thailand. Third, the new states have displayed an increasing tendency to intervene, ordinarily by limited military as well as political means, in internal conflicts and colonial rebellions elsewhere. Examples are the large-scale intervention of the UAR in Yemen, Algeria's aid to the Congo rebels, Cuban support of revolutionaries in Venezuela and other Latin American countries, and the assistance several African states have lent to Angolan rebels. The specific objective of these interventions varies considerably. The support of colonial rebels stems from obvious and powerful motives; and help to foreign insurgents and factions hostile to a politically conservative regime appeals to underdeveloped states governed by radical, socialist, or Communist groups—such as Ghana and Tanzania. But interventionist support may also be based, as it has been frequently in the case of Nasser, on the desire of governments to extend or consolidate their foreign-policy influence over a larger area.

When one considers the large number of states in this category of lesser and non-nuclear powers, large-scale *and* prolonged wars have been remarkably absent during the past two decades. The Chinese attack on India and the encounter between Israel and the UAR in 1956 were of short duration; the 1965 clash between India and Pakistan was rather half-hearted, slightly bizarre, and—

leaving East Pakistan untouched—limited geographically; and the Indonesian attacks on Malaysia were small-scale, sporadic, and curiously one-sided. In part, the limited and short-lived character of these clashes may have been dictated by the fact that these states lack adequate resources to sustain larger-scale, mobile, and distant operations on a conventional military level. At any rate, the military behavior of these nations has been more pugnacious with reference to border skirmishes and support of foreign insurgents, which require far smaller inputs of military resources at any one time.

Nobody can know whether this checkered but not very bellicose record of the recent past will be continued in the future. All we can do is to look for general conditions at this time visible to the analytical eye that are likely to affect relevant behavior. As is understood regarding virtually all propositions in this essay, general tendencies affect, but do not determine, behavior; actual behavior is always subject to a host of particular circumstances, and the members of this large class of nations do of course vary greatly in several basic properties.

Several conditions peculiar to this class of nations fail to restrain resort to international violence or positively favor the generation of interstate conflict within the group. Most of the non-nuclear countries are economically underdeveloped and hence untouched by some of the conditions which operate to deflate the value of territorial conquest in the highly industrialized societies. Many of the less developed countries, moreover, are states of quite recent origin, endowed with political boundaries often fixed arbitrarily by former colonial powers. As part of their colonial heritage, not a few find themselves with boundaries that either divide ethnic communities or envelop several distinct ethnic communities not committed to common nationhood and desirous of setting up a state of their own. Indeed, many of these countries may be said to confront the sort of problems that concerned the now developed countries between 1750 and 1950. Outside of Europe and the Western Hemisphere, there certainly is no dearth of the unsettled boundary conditions that have generated conflict in the past, and will tend to do so in the future. The failure to develop economically may breed frustration, leading to explosive discharges against external foes, and the disposition of leaders with a revolutionary past and bent to succor like-minded revolutionaries elsewhere could lead to the internationalization of internal and local conflicts. Furthermore, the less developed countries have been unable for the most part to build civilian institutions strong enough to control the military. And in their case, no special disincentive arises from the expectations about the costs of military conflict that obtain among the nuclear powers. As long as war is sure to be fought by means of conventional armament, the leaders of the non-nuclear countries do not share the syndrome of fears stimulated by the risks of nuclear war. They do not partake of any nuclear balance of terror. In this very important respect, therefore, they are not affected, at least directly, by some of the recent changes in the nature and utility of war.

However, there also are substantial restraints tending to discourage these states from readily resorting to military aggression against one another. First, some twenty of the lesser and non-nuclear powers have reached the stage of the wealthy modern welfare state, or—as in Eastern and Southern Europe—are approaching that stage; and they exhibit something of the non-aggressive disposition that we analyzed in Chapter III. One does not expect Canada, Switzerland, or Yugoslavia to act as an international aggressor. Second, a good many of the lesser and non-nuclear countries are allies of great and nuclear powers (e.g., members of NATO or the Warsaw Pact); their external policies are controlled to some extent by their more powerful partners, who, being sensitive to the full range of military dangers in the nuclear age, are usually interested in preventing local conflicts in which they might become entangled. Third, the governments of the non-aligned countries, on the other hand, tend to labor under the anxiety that military quarrels between themselves may result in intervention by a great power. Thus, if China were to contemplate large-scale military aggression against India, her government would be justified in foreseeing some chance that the United States, and perhaps other powers, would come to India's aid. The sensitivity to great-power intervention in local conflicts is especially pronounced among leaders of ex-colonial countries, who evidently nurse an abiding fear of imperialist action. Thus, when the United States and Great Britain sent troops into Lebanon and Jordan in 1958, the anxiety of Arab leaders over their states' becoming a battlefield in the "Cold War" spurred their governments to a prompt declaration of solidarity and non-intervention in each other's affairs; and this response facilitated a quick evacuation of British and American forces from the area. Again, the leaders of many African states were strongly opposed to great-power intervention in the Congo's internecine strife. Even if great-power intervention in local fighting were not military, if it involved no more than the interruption of economic assistance, this would be a matter of considerable concern to the government of many poor countries.

Finally, the lesser and non-nuclear countries by and large, and more or less, subscribe to the restraint, in no small measure self-imposed, that is based on the diminished legitimacy of war discussed in Chapter III.

Anyone who studies the speeches made by spokesmen of these countries will be struck by their addiction to this theme. There was no essential difference in the expressions voiced by delegates to the UN from virtually all nations, big or small, developed or underdeveloped, on the occasion of the war between India and Pakistan in 1965. They not only appeared united in demanding a cessation of the conflict, but also exhibited a degree of sorrow and even embarrassment at the sight of the Indians and Pakistanis relapsing into what they seemed to regard as anachronistic and impermissible behavior. The sincerity of these expressions may be doubted by the hard-bitten observer, but such skepticism is not easily substantiated. I myself believe that most of the lesser and non-nuclear nations today have a genuine allegiance to the notion that aggressive war is evil. It is an ingredient in the ideas of Arab or African brotherhood. And to some extent, in fact, this allegiance has found institutional expression in regional organizations, such as the Organization of American States. When a military boundary clash developed between Algeria and Morocco in 1963, the Organization of African Unity was instrumental in bringing about a speedy termination of the conflict.

As we have said repeatedly, restraints are never absolute even when they are strong. They will not override contrary interests when these are sufficiently powerful. But the conditionality of their effectiveness does not deprive them of importance. They are not generally ineffective even though one country, or a few, may resort to war when the stake involved in international conflict is perceived to be of the highest priority. And as history has demonstrated down the centuries, the temptation to shunt restraints aside is greater within any group for the militarily powerful than for the weaker members. It is not accidental that, in the class of countries under consideration, it was China, Indonesia, and India that figured in the few larger-scale conflicts that have taken place since 1945. The other temptation, to which many radical leaders in the underdeveloped world are highly susceptible, is to internationalize internal conflicts and colonial rebellions, and to do so not only within the framework of the United Nations, which has the authority to render internationalization legitimate under certain circumstances, but also through national action in the murky twilight zone of arms smuggling, subversion, infiltration, and political chicanery. To the leaders concerned, their motives may be pure and noble, and action morally indispensable, but the means are apt to be risky to regional and perhaps world peace when they are not guided by accepted international norms and channeled through accepted international or regional institutions. In this respect, the less powerful states can hardly claim exemption from the obligations they wish the powerful states to obey.

CONCLUSIONS ON THE VALUE OF MILITARY POWER

We must now summarize our main conclusions on the value of military power in the nuclear age. It is obvious that, since World War II, there has been a major, if not a dramatic, change in the conception of international war and in the utility of national military power. The usability and utility of military force have undergone a vast transformation, but that the utility of national military power has positively declined we are unable to prove compellingly. The subjective nature of utility does not permit such proof. And yet we want to maintain, and are convinced—intuitively, if in no other way—that there has been a decline in the utility of military power and war, and that this decline has been very substantial, though, as we have also seen, heavily conditioned by a number of factors.

As we saw in Chapter II, the decrease in the usability of military force originated partly in fundamental changes in the ways human societies are organized, and in the post-traditional character and range of human activities and attitudes. These changes commenced long before World War II and are continuing and perhaps gathering strength at present. But it is the advent of nuclear weaponry and its associated sophisticated paraphernalia that have had a truly revolutionary impact on the face of war and on the usability of military power as an instrument of national policy. Certainly, as long as nuclear war spells immense mutual destruction, its costs are grossly disproportionate to any rational objects of foreign policy; and to the extent that a substantial risk of escalation to this excessive level of mutual destruction is inherent in more limited applications of force, their usability has also diminished. The arbitrament of war has become too costly for practically all rational purposes of statecraft, if by "rational" we mean no more than that governments will not choose an action from which, in terms of probabilities, they stand to lose a great deal more than they can hope to gain. As intimated in the introduction of this chapter—and subject to the qualifications stated there—with the decline in the utility of war, particularly large-scale war, the utility of military threats has also decreased, although less than the utility of war; and so has, though probably still less, the utility derived from the mere possession of military forces. As was brought out in the preceding chapters, the value of military capabilities for the essentially defensive purpose of deterrence may not have decreased at all; in fact, it may have risen.

By and large, the behavior of governments has begun

to register the recognition of this change. Both the United States and the Soviet Union have, despite deep tensions and embittered conflicts between them, practiced a policy of war avoidance, and in this sense the balance of terror has resulted in a *Pax Atomica*—precarious though it is, in view of human frailties and the possibility of misunderstanding and blundering. And not all national leaderships have fully comprehended the change. The question of what kind of international war may still be regarded as an acceptable instrument of policy apparently lies at the heart of the bitter Sino-Soviet conflict.[81]

And yet, as long as the world is organized politically as it is, as long as nation-states dispose of the instruments of military force, national military power remains important; it is of some usability and utility. It would be a great error to believe that, in the present world, the possession of military strength is useless, and that the achievement of vital foreign-policy goals can be left entirely to the employment of diplomatic, economic, and moral resources. Surely, a military presence still has its uses. It is not even certain that national capacities for inflicting violence internationally have ceased to be the principal component of international power. But the scope of usability has shrunk radically. The main value of national military power is now its *latent* usability.[82] War is no longer as acceptable a continuation of politics by other means as it once was; but this dictum of Clausewitz and Lenin is not altogether obsolete.

We have also pointed repeatedly to the conditionality of our problem. Thus, mild applications of force are more usable than its massive employment, and even

[81] Cf. Thomas W. Wolfe, *Soviet Strategy at the Crossroads*, Cambridge: Harvard University Press, 1964, pp. 71ff.
[82] Cf. Wohlstetter, p. 9.

sizable limited wars are only conditionally unusable, the critical condition being the danger of escalation to nuclear war between the great nuclear powers. Nuclear capabilities are less usable for most purposes of foreign policy than are non-nuclear forces, but this difference is likewise subject to various conditions. Nor are all nuclear arms alike in their escalatory potential. Whatever utility nuclear military power can still provide, it is subject to differences in national nuclear capabilities, and to the number of nations that have become nuclear powers. But in other respects it is the superpowers that are more subject to restraints on the international use of force than are the non-nuclear and militarily weak nations. And so on.

It is, of course, an important question whether the new conditions now reducing the utility of national military power represent only a temporary development, whether they arise from a constellation of factors that are subject to change. This question is unanswerable. As we pointed out, modern weapons technology remains in flux, and its progress is unpredictable. The development of superbly effective ABM systems would be bound to affect the present balance of terror and impinge on many implications of military power as presently constituted. However, until international disarmament takes place, the enormously destructive power of modern weaponry is not going to diminish, and is likely to increase. And given any substantial uncertainties about the vulnerability of nations—a condition that is likely to prevail—national military power will remain the frightful incubus it has become. It thus remains true that military power has lost practical value at the very time when modern technology has added so large an increment of violence to the military content of power.[83] The crucial fact is that the value of arms lies in their capacity to gain worthwhile objectives; their value does not necessarily rise in proportion to their destructiveness.

[83] Cf. a statement by Stephen King-Hall quoted in Henry E. Eccles, *Military Concepts and Philosophy*, New Brunswick: Rutgers University Press, 1965, p. 31.

CHAPTER VI

SOME EFFECTS ON

INTERNATIONAL RELATIONS

INTERNATIONAL RELATIONS in the 1960's differ in many ways from the international relations of the 1900's or even the 1920's and 1930's. For one thing, the international system is more complex. The rapid process of decolonization created many more actors. The majority of the nation-states are non-"Western," economically underdeveloped, small in population, and inexperienced in government. The leadership of many of these countries looks upon the Western nations, and especially the United States and the great ex-colonial powers, with fear and distrust—some of them indeed displaying a decided anti-Western animus even as their nations are struggling to absorb, and use for their own purposes, Western ideas, knowledge, and capital.

The changed nature of military power, its stupendous capacity to destroy, and the huge costs involved in its employment have impinged heavily on international life. To trace these repercussions systematically would go beyond the modest scope of this essay. But some selected effects and implications will be discussed briefly in the present chapter.

MILITARY POWER AND THE INTERNATIONAL STATUS QUO

Throughout recorded history, violence has served as a major mechanism for changing the intercommunity *status quo*; and intercommunity war, and the threat of such war, have been the major forms in which violence has been employed toward effecting changes in power relationships, in political boundaries, and in the allocation of many values figuring in intercommunity conflicts of interest. But whereas formerly the theater of action was mostly local or regional, now the world has become highly integrated militarily. The reach of national interests and the scale of interstate action are more often global than was the case even a few decades ago. International rivalry is taking place in a "shrunken" world; the scale of nuclear power is global; and the "community of fear"—the fear of involvement in hostilities of unprecedented violence—is likewise global.

Now, to the appreciable extent that military power is less usable in the pursuit of customary foreign-policy goals than used to be the case, the consequences are not evenly distributed among the various powers. According to our conclusion, the great nuclear powers realize that it is too dangerous for them to employ large-scale military force, especially against one another, for the purpose of changing the international *status quo*. The Soviet Union still professes the revolutionary aim of transforming the traditional and existing international order, but its governments have come to deny any intention of using military force for this purpose, except to the extent that they declare their duty and readiness to support "national wars of liberation." They now prefer "peaceful coexistence" with the "capitalist" states, and this preference evidently rests on their desire to conquer by "pacific" means and avoid the risk of all-out nuclear war. Indeed, the Sino-Soviet conflict hinges largely on different concepts in the utility of military power on behalf of world revolutionary goals. The rulers of China agree with the rulers of the Soviet Union that large-scale military war with Western powers should be avoided, but they sharply criticize the Kremlin for paying excessive attention to the business of strategic deterrence and to the danger that local conflicts might escalate to the dreaded strategic level. The Chinese urge the USSR to risk involvement in local conflicts in order to alter the political *status quo*. But even the Chinese act with more circumspection than they speak. The fear of major war does instill caution and tends to make such war too costly as an instrument for altering the *status quo*. And it has been observed that, since 1948, there have been no violent changes in the international *status quo* comparable to those that occurred from 1904 to 1914, or from 1933 to 1939.[84]

The observed caution of the great powers has suggested the inference that the balance of terror does in fact protect the international *status quo*.[85] This consequence would be to the advantage of powers interested in maintaining the present *status quo* and to the disadvantage of those that are eager to revise it. One might then be tempted to argue that this situation benefits the West and works to the detriment of Communist powers which are unwilling to abide by the present order of world politics. The United States might well be regarded as the guardian of the *status quo*. The postwar foreign policy of this country, after all, has been largely defensive. By means of a powerful military posture, a vast network of alliances, and the instrument of foreign economic aid, the United States has attempted to contain Communist expansion, which American governments have perceived as the central menace to an acceptable international order. And in line with our analysis in Chapter II, it

[84] Herbert S. Dinerstein, *The Transformation of Alliance Systems*, RAND Corp. Memorandum P-2993, February 1965, p. 7.

[85] Cf. Aron, *Paix et guerre*, p. 496; Bell, *Negotiations from Strength*, p. 226.

might be suggested that the wealthy, industrial, and predominantly Western nations tend to prefer absorption in the domestic business of the welfare state; that they want essentially to be left undisturbed in the enjoyment of their growing riches; and that they are basically inclined to turn to external affairs only for fundamentally defensive purposes.

However, the argument that the balance of terror preserves the international *status quo* does not, taking the world as a whole, seem to hold water. It would, in fact, be surprising if it did. No particular political status has ever lasted for long, let alone been perpetual. The function of any political order is to distribute objects of value, directly or indirectly, and, whatever an existing system, it is always to the interest or the desire of some people to alter it in order to get more of something. Inevitably, pressures arise, build up, and engender explosive bursts of violence unless change is brought about by gradual adaptation and gentle means. On the international level, even the great powers are therefore unable to stem or control the pressures for change, though they may be able to retard its consummation for a time and to influence somewhat the shape of its consummation, including the modalities of change. But there are several particular reasons for disbelieving that the balance of terror is likely to freeze the international *status quo.*

One of these reasons we have already discussed. Even the balance of terror, particularly if not wholly symmetrical, leaves some room for maneuver, some opportunity for risk-taking, in pressing for revisions in the *status quo.* For example, fear of involvement in an escalating crisis may keep a great nuclear power from taking military action against a small power, or from intervening militarily in a nation engaged in revolutionary strife. But

if such a power overcomes this fear and commits itself to
military action, fear may inhibit escalatory intervention
by another great power. This happened as the United
States deepened its intervention in South Vietnam. It is
said with considerable justification that nuclear deterrence
lends itself to defensive rather than offensive policy purposes, that it affords protection from inroads on the deterring power's value position rather than opportunity
for making inroads on the value position of another nuclear power. But though this reflects a powerful tendency
in the working of mutual nuclear deterrence, it is no more
than a tendency. Its weight may be offset by other factors
in particular situations. In Europe, this tendency has
been reigning supreme for some time, and the balance of
terror has there produced a kind of military *immo-
bilisme*.[86] Outside Europe, however, a welter of political
forces has militated against such stability.

Second, the balance of terror operating among the nuclear powers does not seem to inhibit the behavior of
lesser and non-nuclear countries such as Indonesia and
the UAR; and their military activities might over time
bring about considerable changes in the international
status quo. Third, and probably most importantly, the
balance of terror may not freeze the existing world order
because its inhibiting effects do not extend to all forms of
international violence. Nor, of course, do they extend to
domestic political violence, through which international
relations may also be greatly affected, either cumu-
latively, as many smaller nations change regimes and
leaders in the same political direction, or suddenly when
a large and populous country undergoes revolution, as

[86] Raoul Girardet, "La politique militaire française et l'avenir
des guerres," Bulletin SEDEIS (Société d'études et de docu-
mentation économiques, industrielles et sociales), Paris, February
10, 1965, p. 30.

Russia did in 1917, and China after World War II.

As we have seen, even limited-war forces for employment in local conflict afford only a dangerous form of leverage for the big powers. Yet there are alternative means for upsetting the *status quo,* and these means are at a premium precisely because the usability of military power is restricted to such a narrow scope. The kinds of pressure that escape this constraint are those exerted in "sub-limited" war, in support of local insurrection and terrorism, and through propaganda and revolutionary political appeal; and in war by proxy. The recent shift to these means for revising the *status quo* expresses the depreciation in the value of technologically sophisticated military power. It works to the advantage of states commanding superior resources for these particular activities, and not necessarily of states disinterested in international change.

"SUB-LIMITED WAR"

This new emphasis on capturing states not by full-fledged external aggression but from within, by taking a hand in revolutionary upheaval, and by thus bringing about changes in political alignment, sidesteps formal international conflict, with its heightened risk of destruction and its several other limitations and costs. It breeds practices that in fact have been normal for the Communists and were also, in the 1930's, for the Fascists. Communist ideology is admirably suited to such a policy. The theories of revolutionary conflict developed by Marx and Engels, Lenin and Mao, turn on the irreconcilable antagonism between classes, and this class struggle is, in their eyes, heedless of, and necessarily cuts across, interstate boundaries. The practice of revolutionary warfare blurs the classical distinctions between peace and war, and between civil and international war. To the extent that it gives rise to a new kind of war, it is one in which money, political organization, propaganda, and the simple arms and morals appropriate to assassination, terrorism, and guerrilla war are more indispensable to success than the sophisticated weaponry fashioned for formal and large-scale international conflict. As a Peking spokesman recently declared: "People have come to realize that it is man, and not weapons, that decides the outcome of war. The gunboat is a paper tiger; the aeroplane is a paper tiger; and the atom bomb is likewise a paper tiger."[87] This is a wishful exaggeration, but also a perceptive appraisal. A Western scholar has pointed to the paradox that "though the weapons of mass-destruction grow more and more ferociously efficient, the revolutionary guerrilla armed with nothing more advanced than a rifle and a nineteenth-century political doctrine has proved the most effective means yet devised for altering world power balance."[88]

Washington officials have called this new kind of conflict "sub-limited war"—a most inelegant term, but one that makes an important point. This type of war is often clandestine, more covert than formal war, and aggression is less detectable. Violence, in short, has become less visible and more dispersed and pervasive.[89]

These new conditions go far toward explaining the difficulties recently encountered by the United States in exercising its military power in Southeast Asia and the

[87] Reported in *Global Digest*, II (May 1965), p. 103. See also Lo Jui-ching, "China's Military Doctrine," reprinted from *Red Flag*, in *Survival*, VII (August 1965), pp. 201-7; and the speech by Marshal Lin Piao, the Chinese Defense Minister, in September 1965 (*New York Times*, September 4, 1965, p. 2).

[88] Bell, "Non-Alignment," *op.cit.*, p. 255.

[89] Samuel P. Huntington, "Patterns of Violence in World Politics," in Samuel P. Huntington (ed.), *Changing Patterns of Military Politics*, New York: Free Press, 1962, p. 47.

Far East. These difficulties reflect both the diminished weight of military power in relations between nations of grossly unequal military endowment, and the challenge represented by subversion, infiltration, and insurrection —that is, the intrusion of a political warfare that is associated with peculiarly limited forms of violence and weaponry. The configuration of these conditions accounts for the protracted frustration experienced by the United States, despite the great reach of its military strength, in dealing with Peking, and in trying to contain Communist expansion in Asia.

Communist China has been at great pains not to give the United States any excuse for resorting to its superior military forces. Indeed, she aims to bypass and neutralize this power by employing primarily political weapons that offer no ready targets to military weaponry. They assess and exploit the political susceptibilities of local populations, their anxieties, resentments, and weariness. As George Kennan observes, there "is not one of these places where our own military effort cannot be frustrated, not only deprived of its political meaning but actually rendered physically unsuccessful, if we fail to find support in the temper of the inhabitants."[90] However, the Communists use not only political means. Thus, the Vietcong are numerous enough and armed well enough to conduct a large guerrilla war and widespread terrorism. In 1964 alone, they are reported to have assassinated or kidnapped over 1,500 village chiefs and other government officials.[91] On the other hand, among the various counters it has applied, the United States government sent squadrons of B-52 heavy bombers to practice saturation bombing in South Vietnamese areas suspected of

[90] George Kennan, "A Fresh Look at Our China Policy," *New York Times Magazine*, November 22, 1964, p. 147.
[91] *Time*, May 28, 1965, p. 22.

containing Vietcong bases and troop concentrations. There is a strange and telling contrast in these two types of violence. Indeed, in this vexing situation, the United States has been tempted to "up the ante," to raise the ongoing conflict from a level at which sophisticated military power is of little avail to a level at which that power may find some use. The initiation, in 1965, of bombing raids on North Vietnam and of large ground-force commitments constituted such escalation. Whether it will be progressive, and what its long-run as well as short-run consequences will be, remains to be seen. But there can be little doubt that, in deciding on these moves, the United States government was subject to severe restraints. The usability of its military might is very limited as a result of the factors we have examined in this essay. Walter Lippmann has suggested that the military commitments of the United States on the Asian mainland are overextended.[92] Yet this is surely wrong. If the United States is overextended, it is so not because it faces a strong challenge by military forces similar to its own, but because it is confronted by a form and level of conflict in which its great military power can be brought to bear to a very limited, and possibly inadequate, extent.

Resort to "sub-limited" warfare is attractive for three reasons. It lacks the escalatory risks of limited war; it is a good strategy for the military underdog since it favors nations that lack sophisticated military strength but have mastered the art of political penetration; and it tends to be effective because mankind is passing through a historical phase peculiarly suited to its initiation and conduct. The inhabitants of the vast underdeveloped regions of the world are politically apathetic or restive. Especially in the rapidly growing urban areas and among the multi-

[92] Walter Lippmann, "Globalism and Isolationism," *New York Herald Tribune*, February 23, 1965, p. 26.

plying ranks of the educated, there is a sharpening, even if often ambivalent, dissatisfaction with traditional modes of life. Inevitably, the ongoing process of "modernization" disrupts and dissolves the familiar order of the past, and entails this consequence of destabilization before it proceeds to the stage where a well-structured and well-functioning new order of things has been introduced, has become widely accepted, and hence permits a return to reasonable stability. The transition period is characterized by vast instabilities and by an insufficiency of norms through which social conflict can be settled by peaceful procedures. In this stage, political mobilization advances, often at an explosive pace, but it tends to be accompanied by "political decay" rather than by the quick introduction of institutions that define and promote the common interests of populations.[93] Their capacity for political self-direction is often dubious and inadequate to the novel tasks with which these societies must grapple. Thus rebellions, *coups d'état*, and civil wars are frequent in the less developed areas. In 1965 alone, internal conflicts of this kind occurred in Indonesia, Iraq, the Sudan, Algeria, the Congo, Dahomey, Burundi, Bolivia, and the Dominican Republic, and such instability is likely to persist.

Despite these conditions, the historical record does not show that it is easy to start revolutions and insurrectionary war from the outside. Even most foreign-supported insurrections did not involve the Communists as a major party. Colonial rebellions, as in Algeria and Kenya, were of predominantly local and non-Communist provenance. Nevertheless, the Communist states have been strikingly active and, in Southeast Asia at least, also rather adept at exploiting revolutionary situations. In waging and in

[93] Samuel P. Huntington, "Political Development and Political Decay," *World Politics*, xvii (April 1965), pp. 386-430.

preparing for "sub-limited war," the Communists are able to draw upon some valuable assets. To begin with, they propagate a creed vaguely appealing to some of the leadership in many communities set on rapid development and, by holding out a model for political and economic development, they are often able to tap the new springs of power generated by the "revolution of rising expectations." According to their political model, a few resolute leaders equipped with a set of radical but simple doctrines are able to take on an inchoate political community and weld a nation sufficiently integrated to push speedy economic development. Soviet success with rapid industrialization is, to be sure, of dubious relevance to the problems confronting the underdeveloped areas. When Lenin captured Russia, she had been open to Western ideas, including Western science and technology, for about two centuries, had already undergone considerable economic and industrial development, was a net exporter of food, and was not pressed by a too rapid increase of population. The Chinese example may appear somewhat more apposite, but China also has a cultural and economic heritage more conducive to economic growth than do most of the underdeveloped countries—for example, some fairly advanced industrial complexes in Manchuria and Shanghai, the Chinese propensity to work with discipline and diligence, China's experience of political integration, and her eagerness for literacy and scientific advances. In these matters, however, what counts is not reality but the subjective way in which it is perceived. No doubt, the Communists are deeply committed to "modernization"; and their model is not only of more recent origin, and ideologically simpler, than the liberal-capitalist model that served the West in achieving spectacular progress and, in fact, in pioneering development. Most of the underdeveloped countries lack the peculiar political, social, and cultural preconditions that were the prerequisite of liberal-capitalist development in the West; and a large proportion of the elites, and especially of the intellectuals, in many of these countries are swayed by vague socialist as well as nationalist leanings.[94]

The Communists also display ostentatiously a style of life that is quasi-puritanical, almost ascetic, and clashes conspicuously with the style of traditional rulers or, for that matter, with that of representatives from the affluent societies of the West. The Communist style suggests that its adherents are devoted fanatically to the service of the people rather than to personal or group interest; and this seems to have considerable appeal amidst the poverty that is prevalent in most less developed countries. As we noted in Chapter III, the intellectuals play a key role in much of the underdeveloped world. Having realized this, the Communists make it their business to cultivate what they call the "intelligentsia."[95] Whether deservedly or not, the Communist powers, moreover, have escaped the blemish of an imperialist record and are thus in a position to identify themselves with, and to fan continuously, the anti-imperialist sentiments at large in ex-colonial populations. Of late, Communism also benefits from the resurgence of nationalism in the Communist camp, and from the fact that Moscow has been compelled to make its peace with this development and to accept the claim of Communist states and parties to substantial autonomy, if not complete independence.

As we have already noted, the Communists subscribe to a philosophy geared to the kind of political struggle

[94] Cf. David E. Apter, "Ideology and Discontent," in David E. Apter (ed.), *Ideology and Discontent*, New York: Free Press, 1964, pp. 18ff.

[95] Cf. Ivor Spector, "Russian and Afro-Asian Neutralism," *Current History*, xxxvii (1959), p. 275; Wirjodiatmodjo, *Der Gedanke der Blockfreiheit*, pp. 93ff.

that cuts across political boundaries while shunning the method of formal international war. The Chinese leaders particularly see world politics as moving under their leadership to a gathering and irresistible revolution against what they call the capitalist-imperialist power complex, and against the United States as its major citadel. They think it is their duty to help destroy the old established order and they are unencumbered by a genuine acceptance of the system of nation-states and of the traditional rules governing their international behavior. As, for instance, in Mao's teachings, they have evolved an integrated strategy that capitalizes on these assets.[96] This strategy directs political appeal and maneuver with a ruthlessness that is completely unhampered by "bourgeois" scruples.

These assets in the pursuit of "indirect aggression" should not be exaggerated. Considering the enormous efforts invested by the Communists in these activities, their record does not so far add up to dramatic success. It has, for example, been singularly unsuccessful in the Middle East. The Soviet Union particularly has had some disillusioning experiences; and it has not in recent years done its utmost to promote the world revolution.[97] —a fact which Peking has been quick to notice and decry. Perhaps the Soviet leaders have convinced themselves that the present world situation is not ripe for rapid revolutionary advances and they are simply biding their time until circumstances are more propitious. But in Eastern Europe and the USSR one also senses a decline of missionary zeal, a certain fatigue of ideology. Communism is, after all, by now an aging revolutionary movement. In

[96] Cf. Tang Tsou and Morton H. Halperin, "Mao Tse-tung's Revolutionary Strategy and Peking's International Behavior," *American Political Science Review*, LIX (March 1965), pp. 80-99.
[97] Bell, "Non-Alignment," *op.cit.*, pp. 255f.

most of the underdeveloped world, the rising leadership, although inclined to borrow ideas as well as receive aid from left and right, is addicted to home-grown brands of nationalism and socialism; it is far from eager to align with any of the major power blocs. And as the world becomes more familiar with Communist intrigue abroad, and with the record of Communist rule and its blessings, more people will notice a marked discrepancy between practice and ideal.

Nevertheless, Chinese militancy remains unabated. The Communist appeal will tend to be powerful where corrupt and inept leadership prevails, and where frustrations are strong enough to propel a minority to revolutionary action while keeping the majority of the population from giving the incumbent government effective support. And, if it comes to protracted internal war, Communist intervention will be especially potent in areas contiguous to the Communist states. In such areas —and South Vietnam is one of them—military power alone will not suffice to beat back the Communist offensive. What will be indispensable are political resources that are adapted to the case on hand; and this means political resources that are primarily local. In these cases, the United States cannot hope for more than a margin of political influence. It represents a part of the world that is rich, white, and utterly alien.

It is not clear that there is a feasible American answer to "national wars of liberation" in which conditions favor Communist intervention. The difficulty is to know at the start of a local crisis, involving Communist intervention from outside, whether conditions are or are not favorable. The number of conditions critical to Communist success, and the failure of many a Communist attempt, suggest that one should be wary of generalizations on this matter, which is not only exceedingly complex but also subject to more or less unique local circumstances; and though a local will to resist hostile foreign intrusion is crucial, local resources may be inadequate for success. Assisting the local resistance is not necessarily useless or illegitimate. It is all very well to note, from the viewpoint of long historical perspective, that every expansionist threat sooner or later stimulates the development of countervailing local forces. The trouble is that their development takes time and that a great deal of damage may have been done before a new international balance of forces emerges and aggressive expansion is halted. It may therefore make sense for other powers to step in, if they have the interest and the capability, in order to provide the time required for local forces to develop sufficient alertness and strength. But it is equally clear that not every situation of "sub-limited war" is susceptible to successful assistance from the outside. United States support can be decisive where a minority of Communist-supported insurgents challenge a basically stable local system. Where this condition is absent, the sheer insertion of military power from outside is costly in various ways, including some risk of escalating conflict; and it is unlikely to succeed. Thus, the international *status quo* could change appreciably and violence and "indirect aggression" may well play a significant part in producing the change; but the kind of military strength designed for formal international war is apt to be an asset of limited, if not dubious, value.

MILITARY ALLIANCES

The present international system abounds in military alliances. In 1965, the United States had 42 allies and the Communist camp encompassed 12 states (including Cuba), each alliance complex comprising roughly a third of the world's population. In addition, there are special alliances maintained by the lesser nuclear powers and, of course, a number of regional and local alliances formed by non-nuclear states. The question arises whether the modified nature of war and the changes in the usability of national military forces do not have a significant bearing on the worth and functioning of alliances.

Of course, alliances differ greatly in the numbers and properties of their members, and in the purposes they are meant to serve. Like the possession and use of military power by nations, alliance membership involves a variety of advantages and disadvantages. Among the possible "costs" are the risk of being drawn into the conflicts of allies, a curtailed freedom of action in certain matters of foreign policy, and perhaps even of domestic policy, the need to give economic aid to poorer allies, and so on. Among the possible gains are increased security, augmented power to pursue aggressive ends, savings in national defense expenditures, prestige, and the receipt of material aid. Presumably, an alliance is formed and maintained if the gains expected by members over time exceed, or at least match, the anticipated disadvantages. The value and functioning of particular alliances depend, of course, on relationships among particular allies with reference to particular conflict situations, actual or contingent. But this essay is concerned only with selected general conditions in the nuclear age that tend to affect alliances. Indeed, its focus will be on alliances in which at least one member is a nuclear power.

We may infer from the preceding analysis that two general conditions tend to reduce the value of such (and perhaps other) alliances in the nuclear age. First, to the extent that military power is now less usable, because of either its more restricted legitimacy or the risk of escalation, alliances should be somewhat less valuable than they used to be. The restraints involved are, as we pointed

out, highly conditional and hence a precarious basis for
security, but they increase the feasibility of neutrality
and non-alignment. And they are backed, as we also
suggested, by the rivalry of the superpowers, which may
induce them to come to the aid of a country even if it be
not an ally. Thus, if France were to opt out of NATO, she
might still receive protection by the United States in
any serious confrontation with the Soviet Union because
to provide this protection would be in the continuing
interest of the United States. Similarly, when India was
threatened militarily by China, she received considerable support from both the United States and the Soviet
Union even though she was not an ally of either great
power. Second, if all kinds of international wars have
become more risky because they involve, or may lead to
the involvement of, nuclear powers on both sides, then
allies of nuclear powers share in this risk of suffering
colossal devastation. This expectation should also tend to
render such alliances less desirable. However, in order to
illumine these relationships further, we must make some
distinctions. Allies may be great or small powers, nuclear
or non-nuclear states, developed or underdeveloped
countries. These variable properties make a difference.

To begin with the nuclear superpowers, which are the
kingpins of the large alliance systems, there are several
factors that tend to make alliances less advantageous to
them than alliances were for great powers before 1945.
First, allies now add decidedly less to the security of a
great power against the direct attack of another. To be
sure, allied forces and resources, territory, and geographic
location are still important in limited, non-nuclear wars.
But it is improbable that such wars will be massive,
protracted, and crucial between coalitions actively including a nuclear superpower on each side. On the
other hand, non-nuclear allies will add next to nothing to

the defense of the superpowers against a strategic assault, or to the deterrence of such an attack. A lesser ally equipped with nuclear weapons of its own may somewhat contribute to deterrence, and hence to the security of the superpower. The very existence of such a nuclear ally may complicate the strategic plans and operations of the adversary superpower and divert some of its strike force. (This is of little import as long as the hostile superpower has redundant capabilities or is equipped with shorter-range weapons capable of hitting the ally but not the more distant superpower.) All of this reflects the central facts that the gulf in military strength between a great nuclear and a non-nuclear power is far wider than the normal power discrepancies known in previous ages; that offensive arms are decisively superior to defensive weapons; and that intervening space between antagonists affords little protection to either. Therefore, traditional balance-of-power considerations are now less likely to make allies attractive to a great nuclear power. These considerations now recommend self-dependence—that is, dependence on the great power's own economic capacity and growth, on its own military effort, and especially also on its own military research and development.

Second, non-nuclear allies, being extremely exposed to nuclear threats and attacks, are wholly dependent for their protection from these on the deterrent capacity of their nuclear ally. It follows that the latter must be willing to risk its own vulnerable cities and populations as long as the present nuclear standoff between the Big Two prevails, although actually this risk is likely to vary greatly and may often be quite small. The opposing nuclear power will not be deterred from attacking or blackmailing the non-nuclear ally of the other—supposing it wished to do so—unless it foresees some possibility, though not necessarily a great one, that the other super-power will risk its cities in order to protect its ally. This in itself, surely, makes a non-nuclear ally a considerable liability, and makes it hard to give a completely credible nuclear guarantee to an ally. This risk is increased if there is some possibility that non-nuclear allies, pursuing a risky foreign policy of their own, will provoke tensions and conflicts in which the danger of escalation is inherent and in which their nuclear ally may become entangled. The obligation to intervene may then be extremely inconvenient.

Third, in view of their own military unimportance, or anyhow their scant ability to bolster appreciably the deterrent power of the alliance, lesser and non-nuclear allies may develop a propensity for shifting the military burden as much as possible onto the big nuclear ally, and especially to neglect making a feasible contribution to defense against non-nuclear attack. They are apt to rationalize this position by claiming an alliance posture of strategic nuclear deterrence as the best strategy for coping with all, even very limited, kinds of aggression. Thus the gross differences in feasible contributions tend to favor a policy of excessive military dependence on the big ally. Moreover, in the case of underdeveloped and poor countries, allies may require sizable and prolonged aid in order to build up and sustain their military strength; this constitutes another drain on the resources of the big power. Yet countries that make a dispro-portionately small contribution to the military worth of an alliance, or become an economic burden on the stronger partner, will not necessarily be modest in importuning the latter.

Finally, any limits on the big ally's freedom of decision-making are especially onerous and dangerous in confrontations with a nuclear opponent. Although predominant nations have rarely been free from the restraining intervention of their allies, and also from the restraint produced by anticipating such intervention, this is a serious handicap in the nuclear age whenever fateful military decisions must be made. For one thing, since all-out nuclear war can erupt at, or without, a moment's notice, crisis decisions must usually be made without delay and hence do not tolerate the time-consuming process of interallied consultation and negotiation toward the development of consensus. This is quite different from the pre-nuclear era when war usually evolved gradually, after its outbreak, through progressive mobilization, and decisive battles occurred seldom in the first few days of hostilities. In the course of several tense crises over Berlin, the United States had great difficulty in getting allied agreement on the countermoves of the West. On the other hand, it is interesting to note in this respect that the NATO allies of the United States played no part in solving the Cuban missiles crisis of 1962; and this concentration of decision-making also apparently took place on the other side. In so fast-moving and dangerous a crisis, no time and energy could be spared for interallied conferences. And the importunity of allies may not only cause delay; they may also press for particular and mutually contradictory decisions. Compromise decisions reflecting the conflicting interests of allies may be inadequate militarily and, particularly in terms of effective deterrence, give rise to uncertainty and misunderstanding by the opponent when certainty and comprehension are of the essence. Compromise decisions could be dangerously fateful. And regarding crisis decisions of a less technical military character—decisions involved in the give and take of crisis bargaining with the opponent—the clashing interests of allies can also be an obvious disadvantage. The fact is that in a dangerous crisis it is precisely the two adversary superpowers that may have a common interest in finding a way of accommodation, or in tolerating a deadlock, in order to avoid escalation. They may then discover that any specific steps required for this purpose run counter to the interests of an ally. For example, in de-escalating the Cuban missiles crisis, the Soviet government apparently had considerable trouble in securing Castro's cooperation.

None of these drawbacks of alliance materialize of necessity in every crisis. On the contrary, disagreement among allies can also produce benefits. The criticism of allied governments may contain good advice, and may be recognized as such after proper scrutiny; their pressure may prevent hasty and ill-considered action; and occasionally, in bargaining with the adversary, the big ally may be able to turn the disagreement of allies to diplomatic advantage. Obviously, the balance of drawbacks and disadvantages depends on particular circumstances. But even a considerable probability that the balance will be harmful to the big ally in encounters with another great nuclear power will be a matter of serious concern.

Thus, in the nuclear age, alliances entail serious and sobering drawbacks to the great nuclear powers. However, there are counterconsiderations of substantial weight. First, and as already intimated, non-nuclear allies can be of appreciable advantage to a nuclear superpower in the event of limited and also "sub-limited" war. For use in such conflicts, non-nuclear allies may well have suitable forces and supplies, transportation facilities, and bases. Second, and more important, the superpowers may have a variety of interests in protecting other countries. In addition to the claims of previous legal commitment, these interests may derive from historical association, common bonds of culture and ideology, economic affiliations, care for the well-being of other communities, and the appreciation of other qualities which such nations possess and the continued presence of which makes up a "compatible world," and the prerequisite for fashioning a world order in which it is easy, profitable, and un-dangerous to live with one's neighbors. Similarly, it is in the interest of a superpower to confine its opponent's military and political sway, the expansion of which would probably mean not only a shrinking of the "compatible world" but also, in the longer run, significant additions to the resources that the adversary great power might be able to expend on increasing the military pres-sure at its command. In this connection, alliances have a specific instrumental value to the superpowers. By establishing and maintaining an alliance with a lesser power, they undertake a military commitment serving notice on the other superpower that the value at stake in any conflict over the ally concerned, and its territory, is great enough to conjure up the risk of a clash highly dangerous to both. The power to deter is thus invested in a particular commitment; and furthermore, treaty obli-gations make it easier for the big ally to intervene in international conflicts of interest to it.

We can be brief in discussing the merits and demerits of alliance in the nuclear age as seen from the vantage point of the militarily lesser ally; the points involved are mostly a reflection of those examined with reference to the position of the nuclear superpowers. To the lesser power, alliance with a great power may now seem less worthwhile because of doubts over the latter's readiness in a grave emergency to accept the risk of colossal de-struction for the sake of lending protection to an ally. Any demands lesser allies may make for sharing in the control of the nuclear capabilities of the nuclear ally are likely to be rejected in view of the latter's concern that allied veto power would paralyze decision-making in time of utmost peril.

Lesser allies may also suffer from the anxiety that, facing an enormously riskful decision, the nuclear ally may prefer making concessions at the expense of its allies. On the other hand, they may worry about the possibility of becoming involved in, and suffering mutilation in, a nuclear war over the genesis of which they had no control. Lesser allies may also be irritated by the control over their military and foreign policies which the superpower claims in its own interest of avoiding dangerous conflicts with the other great nuclear power. At the same time, they may also be given to the view that the chances of aggression against them have decreased to negligible proportions as an automatic result of the danger that any military clash between the superpowers is apt to escalate to a level it is in the strongest interest of both to avoid and that they will therefore also avoid any aggressive moves against lesser powers that might engender such a clash. Finally, lesser allies may conclude that the allied superpower has in any case so powerful an interest in affording them protection that this interest would survive the demise of formal alliance —that is to say, that substantial security can be obtained without paying the price of alliance.

But there is one solid item on the credit side. A lesser and non-nuclear power is wholly unable to find through its own efforts military security against an aggressive nuclear superpower. Reduced to its own resources, its position is militarily hopeless. As long as it is subject to an overwhelming threat, actual or contingent, the alternatives to alliance with a superpower are few, risky, and costly. It may seek precarious refuge in a stance of "neutralism" or in pursuing a placatory policy toward the great power that presents an actual or latent threat. If in possession of adequate potential resources, it may consider becoming a nuclear power itself in order to rely, in part at least, on its own capacity to deter. As was demonstrated in Chapter IV, this is also, at least for most lesser nations, a tenuous basis for security. Surely, the value of the nuclear capabilities under development in France and China depends in no small measure on the backing these nations might receive respectively from the United States and the Soviet Union.

Alliances have therefore not lost attraction, although their attractiveness will obviously vary, in addition to other circumstances, with the way governments estimate the threat to their security, and this may depend upon geographic location and other particulars. To the middle powers, alliance with a superpower is bound to seem more dubious an asset than to countries of lesser size and resources. In most instances, the present middle powers (Britain, France, Germany, Japan) have enjoyed the rank of great power until very recently; they will find any claim by an allied superpower to exercise control over their foreign and military policies especially vexing, if not wholly obnoxious. The costs of alliance may loom large in the eyes of their governments. They also have—or their leaders imagine that they have—a sufficient resource base for becoming a respectable nuclear power on their own. It is not surprising, therefore, that France became an increasingly uneasy and obstreperous member of NATO in the 1960's, that Communist China aggressively asserted its independence from Moscow, and that both chose to become independent nuclear powers.

The alliance of an underdeveloped country with one of the superpowers, or with any of the larger industrial nations, may not only have the advantage of augmenting security from the external threat specified by the *casus foederis*, but also of placing the country in a favorable position for soliciting and receiving economic aid and technical assistance from its wealthier partner. On the other hand, many ex-colonial countries are at present rather allergic to alliance with an ex-imperial or with any great power, are loath to identify with the East-West conflict, and prefer their vaunted posture of non-alignment. Indeed, an underdeveloped country may assume some special disadvantages if it allies itself with the United States or any of the larger Western nations. It may lose the advantage of receiving economic favors from both superpowers. If it is politically unstable, and especially if it is torn by internal strife, it may become a target of Communist infiltration and subversion. Such indirect aggression tends to be particularly virulent in the case of countries having a common boundary with a Communist state, as in Southeast Asia, or with a state in which Communist influence is strong. Such an ally might furthermore labor under the disadvantage that its government is easily branded as puppet of an imperialist power by its domestic opposition as well as by Communist and "neutralist" nations.

The new facts of international life may well cause nations to review the merits of alliance. Always depending upon circumstances, the superpowers may come to prefer to formal alliance in many an instance the extension of some sort of security guarantee, or symbolizing in some other way their readiness to give support in certain kinds of emergency. In fact, from the viewpoint of the superpowers, it is hard to see why genuine non-alignment on the part of militarily feeble states should not look very attractive. Such countries could be helped if an occasion of distress arose, and this without need to undertake commitments that in the future might turn out to be awkward. Similarly, and again depending on special circumstances, lesser powers might become confirmed in their preferences for non-alignment, especially as long as there is likelihood that the superpowers will police each other as well as the middle powers, and if the United Nations and regional organizations were to demonstrate some capacity for confining, subduing, and terminating, if not altogether deterring, conflict. The major disadvantage of such preferences for either kind of power is, of course, the greater ambiguity of commitment which is necessarily the price to be paid for the avoidance of rigid commitment.

EQUALITY AND INEQUALITY OF INTERNATIONAL POWER

It has been claimed that the international system of nation-states has recently exhibited a trend toward a lesser inequality of power—we should say: of usable power. Various observers have alleged that, though the power structure of the system was highly bipolar in the period immediately following World War II, it has since turned more loosely bipolar, or is in the process of becoming "multipolar" or "polycentric," or indeed has essentially ceased to be bipolar.[98]

If by "bipolarity" we mean "the concentration of most of the world's power" (military, industrial, and otherwise) in two "superpowers" as "the major determinants of world politics,"[99] then we can readily agree that the actual distribution of international power in the late 1940's and early 1950's approximated the description of the bipolar pattern; and it is easy to arrive at the impression that the world of interstate power and influence was less bipolar in 1960 than in 1950, and still less so in 1965. However, the debate on whether the present pattern

[98] E.g., Roberto Ducci, "The World Order in the Sixties," *Foreign Affairs*, LXII (April 1964), p. 388.

[99] Herz, *International Politics in the Atomic Age*, p. 29.

still is or has stopped being bipolar seems doomed to be rather fruitless, for the concept of bipolarity does not specify or suggest criteria on the basis of which one could specify with which configuration in the real world bipolarity ends and something else begins. Although the term "bipolarity" was descriptively very suggestive after the end of World War II, when four powers that had been counted among the select number of great powers only a few years before were utterly exhausted and the defeated ones politically prostrate, and all vastly outranked by the two superpowers of near-continental size; and although many nations then aligned themselves in defense against the threat emanating from, or believed to emanate from, a monolithic Communist bloc, the concept soon ceased to yield more than a partial and superficial impression of international reality. Fixation on this concept began to obscure the many changes taking place in the interstate system.

The purpose of this essay is not to trace, let alone explain, the changing patterns of international influence. The kinds and bases of international influence, coercive and non-coercive, are many; and many changes that are the outcome of unique circumstances modify the international position of particular states without necessarily altering discernible patterns of influence distribution throughout the world. Our more modest task is to offer some observations on changes in military-power relations, and thus point out some implications of the preceding analysis.

This task is greatly facilitated if we distinguish between *gross* military resources—that is, the relative military capabilities possessed by states—and *effective* military power—that is to say, the military strength that can be employed without the entailment of substantial, if not prohibitive, costs and thus tends to make its weight felt in international conflicts. Effectiveness turns on usability; and usability is a matter of degree and subject to the conditions we have examined. A nation may maintain large and expensive forces, but its ability to exert military pressure on other nations must obviously depend on the latter's expectation that these forces are likely to be used. Existing military forces, to be sure, *can* be used, and this fact will yield a degree of power—latent and even actual; but the question at issue is one of probabilities of employment. These probabilities are confined by the various costs and restraints identified in this essay.

Starting with the superpowers, their strategic nuclear capabilities are eminently useful as long as other powers dispose of a nuclear threat. But as long as the balance of terror prevails, their utility is exhausted in deterrence of a direct attack and, as we have seen, in discouraging each other from pursuing courses of action that the other may oppose and that therefore introduce the risk of dangerous escalation. This power to deter, and its manipulation in a crisis situation, is even greater when a superpower confronts a lesser nuclear power, except of course that its superiority may be checkmated by the interventionist threat of the other superpower.

There have been assertions that nuclear weapons have a tendency to level differences in military power between states. Thus, one American commentator avers that the nuclear bomb, "like the gun, may be described as the great equalizer," that is, it "gives the small and the weak the same chance and power to destroy as the big and the strong."[100]

This is a dubious contention, if not an erroneous one. It may be true that, if a small nuclear power has enough capacity to threaten a non-nuclear country with de-

[100] Joseph Newman, "The Red and the Dead," *New York Herald Tribune*, September 4, 1965, p. 8.

struction, and commands the ruthlessness actually to loose nuclear weapons on a non-nuclear opponent, it is in a sense the equal of a big nuclear power, or even superior if the latter lacks the ruthlessness. This is, however, a very "iffy" proposition. Even if the small nuclear power mustered the requisite ruthlessness, it might have to fear, and might be restrained by, the possible intervention of other nuclear powers. On the other hand, whether a "small" nuclear power has strategic capabilities sufficient in number, invulnerability, and penetration force to checkmate a big nuclear power in terms of deterrence is ultimately an empirical question—though one for obvious reasons not subject to easy empirical proof. If it has that capability, it is a great nuclear power. Yet, for reasons indicated in Chapter IV, it is improbable that the nuclear bomb will generally figure as the "great equalizer." Though one may concede that many countries now have or will soon acquire the resources to become some sort of nuclear power, one expects significant differences in national nuclear power to evolve. It is one thing for a country to procure a small and relatively primitive nuclear capability; it is quite another to afford the number of highly sophisticated weapons, the complex strategic infrastructure, and the ability to engage in the probably continuous arms innovation that the superpowers are able to sustain. Let us not forget that, up to 1965, even the Soviet Union was unable to match the strategic military power of the United States. Its comparatively smaller resource base was in all likelihood a major factor in this outcome.

Class differences in military nuclear strength may not correspond to fine differences in national economic products or national product per capita, if only because nations differ in their determination to allocate resources to the military sector, and in the skill with which these resources are transformed into military strength. But gross differences in national income, in technology and scientific resources, and in size of country and population will count. The restraint imposed by a paucity of resources will be felt especially in underdeveloped countries experiencing rapid population growth. As one Indian politician is reputed to have exclaimed: "China's best bomb is the Indian baby." It may also be assumed that though some countries may be able to procure nuclear weaponry from abroad, this is no way to become a great nuclear power. To judge on the basis of present evidence, it will be hard, and rare in practice, for even a middle power—say, France or Britain—to develop and maintain in the face of continuing technological innovation a national nuclear capability sufficiently threatening to a superpower to act as an "equalizer." If it does happen, the power concerned will have become a great nuclear power by dint of exceptional resources, determination, and ingenuity.

It is nevertheless true that by obtaining a nuclear capability of some military consequence, a middle power becomes less unequal vis-à-vis a superpower than it was before; and it stands to gain correspondingly vis-à-vis non-nuclear middle powers, and vis-à-vis small powers, whether nuclear or non-nuclear. But should the world come to be blessed with twenty or thirty or even more countries disposing of nuclear bombs, they will not be military equals.

But these are still considerations referring to gross military capabilities. The extent to which gross military strength can be turned into effective military power depends notably on the following general conditions. First, it depends upon the skill with which the threat of resorting to force is introduced in interstate bargaining; and this depends, among other things, on how other forms of coercive and especially of non-coercive influence are combined with military pressure. The complementary use of non-military forms of influence—such as international respect and diplomatic concessions—depends both on the varying supplies of these resources and on the skill with which the "power package" is designed in concrete instances. Second, the transformation of gross strength into effective military power is affected by the comparative propensity of leaders to gamble and to run risks that can be enormous in the nuclear age. Third, the transformation is influenced by the sensitivity of governments to the other restraints we have examined— that is, the narrowed legitimacy of war, the stigma currently attached to nuclear weapons, and the other conditions that permit, if not encourage, small countries to stand up against vastly stronger powers. Fourth, the effectiveness of military power depends upon the technological suitability of national force structures to employment in particular types of conflict. Thus, since much of the military capability of the superpowers is specialized to the mission of mutual confrontation and deterrence, and largely unusable in conflicts with lesser and non-nuclear powers, the military superiority of the superpowers over lesser powers is less formidable than a comparison of military budgets would suggest. This superiority is still further diminished by the facts that the costs of transmitting military power over great distances still apply to conventional forces, and that conventional forces do not enjoy the stupendous mobility and striking speed characteristic of nuclear weapon systems. These "equalizing" tendencies apply *a fortiori* to the military means at a premium in "sub-limited war"; and these are wars in which the productivity of military force is highly conditioned by associated political resources. The United States fighting guerrillas in South

Vietnam is a great power, but it is a great power fighting under extraordinary handicaps. We must distinguish between different levels and locales of violence in comparing the military might of nations.

As a result of such conditioning factors, the picture of effective relations of military power is not nearly as clear as implied either in the concept of bipolarity, or in the concept of the nuclear bomb as the "great equalizer." We may, however, suggest the following conclusions.

First, the principal military powers tend to be states that are highly industrialized and have greatly differentiated governmental and military structures. The superpowers at present excel all others in the breadth and depth of their resource base. Despite her huge population, the acumen and drive of her leadership, and other assets, Communist China is not a principal *military* power at this time. The assets that are hers make her superior militarily to any other country on the Asian mainland. But although China has more than 120 million men of military age and maintains large military forces, she is militarily strong vis-à-vis the superpowers only if these refrain from using nuclear weapons, and even then only within the confines of her own territory and the immediate periphery, not too remote from her main industrial base in Manchuria.

Second, the great risk involved in any direct military clash between them has induced the superpowers to prefer safer means for acting out their antagonism as well as their half-hearted attempts at bringing about a *détente*. They are engaged in a war of words, a spectacular arms race, a conspicuous rivalry for prestige in outer-space activities, and in diplomatic competition by means of wielding the foreign-aid instrument.

Third, the military power which the superpowers are able to organize and manage has somewhat diminished because their alliance systems have recently lost cohesion and solidarity—a development to be explained in part by the loss in effective military power suffered by the two superpowers. In this respect, the Sino-Soviet split weighs more heavily on the USSR than the French desire for maximum autonomy bothers the United States. But there is a tendency on both sides to pay less heed to, and be more critical of, the dominant military power.

Fourth, concerning limited and particularly "sub-limited" war, the international system is more pluralistic in terms of capabilities than it appears to be at a quick and superficial glance. Certainly effective military power for waging such struggles is much more diffused than is suggested by the international distribution of gross military capabilities in all its forms. It is precisely for this reason that Communist China has been able to wield in Asia a degree of effective military power quite out of proportion to its modest rank in terms of gross military power.

Fifth, the world has become safer, though not of course completely safe, for small powers than it was prior to the nuclear age. This increment in safety, however, is less effective in affording security from aggressive acts by other small powers than from military attack or reprisal by medium and great powers. The various restraints identified in this essay seem to rest more heavily on the big industrialized nations, and especially on the Western military powers, than on poorer and non-Western countries. The widespread adherence to a posture of non-alignment manifests a strong tendency to deny great military powers the advantage of their superior strength—indeed, to cast doubts on the legitimacy of its exercise. This tendency is also manifest in repeated attempts by lesser powers to seal off local areas of conflict from great-power intrusion.

Sixth, a by-product of the changes we have described has been an alteration both grossly and subtly in the balance of usability, and utility, between military and non-military instruments of statecraft. Negotiation in its various forms, the use of economic support and denial, the exploitation of international respect, the manipulation of ideological symbols—in short, all non-military bases of international influence—have gained in value as resort to military force has become hemmed in by a number of restrictions and discouraged by a variety of costs, including the risk of mutual destruction on a monstrous scale. Some of these other bases of international influence—notably, the capacity for extending economic aid—rest on the same economic, technological, and scientific resources that also feed gross military strength, and hence are distributed along a similar pattern. This is not true, or much less true, of some of the other forms of influence. The adroit communication of political attitudes, ideas, and symbols is facilitated by kinds of skill and knowledge that are widely diffused through the world. In fact, one discerns here an advantage that the elites in the underdeveloped world have over their counterparts in the wealthy industrial countries. The former have a keener insight into the political forces agitating and revolutionizing their troubled part of the world. They are closer to its problems. This sharper and surer knowledge gives them an edge when it comes to guiding, exploiting, or even perverting these forces; and it is an edge that can be translated into political strength and influence. The conscious use of this strength counts today for more than military strength in many conflict situations. It is indeed one of the causes of the relative decline in the effectiveness of gross military strength.

But we must re-emphasize that, the various restraints on the employment of military power notwithstanding, national military force has not ceased to be a most important reality in the interstate system. Though brutal and large applications of military force are of diminished serviceability in many situations, and the skillful use of small doses of sophisticated force as well as the employment of other forms of international influence have risen in value, they remain useful in others. No doubt, the military power of nation-states greatly varies according to circumstance. And it is exactly this conditionality of the problem that defies any attempt to draw hard and fast lines between usability and nonusability or to design formulas for extracting from gross military capabilities a maximum of effective military power. All we can be sure of is that the restraints on its use are variable but real, and that they are not absolute. As long as gross military strength exists, it can always be used; and this possibility affects international relations. Although small powers are now safer than they used to be from being cruelly bullied or justly chastised by the superior might of big powers, they are not absolutely safe; and hence they lack neither respect for, nor fear of, military superiority.

Even though national military power now imposes on mankind the nightmarish possibility of catastrophic destruction, it continues to act as an indispensable mainstay of international order as we know it. To appreciate this fact, we need only imagine what would happen if, say, the United States, or Israel, suddenly decided to disarm itself unilaterally. If military power is at a discount in some uses, and hobbled in certain types of international confrontation, this is compatible with great effectiveness, for instance, in deterring nuclear aggression. The fact that this world—rife with tensions and replete with conflicts—has witnessed a great deal of violence but no use of nuclear weapons, and no declaration of war, since 1945, may result, in an obscure and complicated way, from both the usability of gross military power and the remarkable restraints on its use.

These concluding remarks are not intended to summarize my findings on the subject. Any attempt at a brief and comprehensive summary would be bound to fail. Most of the findings are hypotheses, most of the observations offered depend upon personal judgment, and neither hypotheses nor observations are capable of easy verification. The subject is ineluctably complex; every analytical focus, though indispensable to enhanced understanding, suffers from the usual shortcomings of abstraction; and the presentation cannot help but lose from the impossibility of saying everything at once.

THE IMPAIRMENT OF NATIONAL SECURITY

By way of a final word, it seems opportune to return to the opening theme of this essay. Throughout recorded history, provision of security from military threat and assault has been the traditional function of the military forces or levies of tribes, principalities, cities, and nations. The security which could be achieved by these means was, over time, always demonstrably precarious since it could be breached by superior hostile force. Tribes were not seldom driven from their domain, enslaved or literally exterminated, cities sacked, and principalities and nations ravaged. Yet recent military technology has added a new measure of insecurity with which nations must put up. Even the largest and wealthiest countries are vulnerable to nuclear attacks capable of inflicting catastrophic devastation. For example, if arms technology had not progressed beyond the 1939 level, the United States and the Soviet Union would be at present invulnerable to a mortal blow to their military security. To be sure, resort to military force is now subject to the various restraints we have identified. But the risk of dangerous conflagration remains and, since this includes the risk of mortal mass destruction, national security is hollow at its base and mankind subsists under an unprecedented dimension of terror. The present fact is that, over the long run, the military technology symbolized by the nuclear bomb and the intercontinental ballistic missile must be regarded as incompatible with security under the existing international order.

As their sensitivity to the new restraints indicates, national leaders have begun to adapt themselves to the revolutionary change that has occurred. But it is hardly arguable that adaptation has gone far enough as long as the risk of nuclear mass destruction persists. This risk can be diminished, but it cannot be eradicated, under the traditional mode of organizing military force. The untrammeled freedom of nations to provide themselves with the military capabilities they care to have, and the merely rudimentary restraints on their free use of these forces, look like an outmoded license. Since it is impossible to revert to a more traditional technology, the militarily sovereign nation-state is an anachronism.

It is evidently easier to invent new weapons under national auspices than to establish a new international order, and the military structure to support it. To create such an order requires that mankind, in its divided parts, act in relevant respects like a community. Only a marriage of sufficient consensus and sufficient power can beget an order from which the nuclear nightmare is banished. It is the supreme and tragic dilemma of our time that this prerequisite is not in sight. Disarmament conferences, and UN Assembly resolutions denouncing the use and spread of nuclear weapons, may turn out to be precursors of an enterprise aimed at a revolutionary transformation of the world's political organization. Thus far, however, they have made only slight inroads on an urgent problem while, in the meantime, governments follow their customary practice of squaring off in the pursuit of clashing policies, although the conflict posture of the great nuclear powers is subdued by their desire to avoid the risks of a dangerous showdown.

Not a few leaders and not a few of their followers are undoubtedly alert to the basic insecurity that now prevails, and some undoubtedly feel the impulse to seek escape from the present impasse by "modernizing" an ancient structure of political relationships that is unable to cope with a runaway technology—that is to say, with a situation brought about by the uncritical acceptance of technological innovation. However, though utopias are certainly not lacking, there is no obvious way out of the trap that man has ingeniously constructed around himself. It is not only that any course that might be charted is full of uncertainties, riskful to national security and the values it is meant to protect, and in all likelihood irreversible. It is also that political institutions and behavior are far less fluid than scientific knowledge and technological capabilities. Most people anywhere are plainly unwilling, and indeed unable, to question and discard established modes of social existence and practice. While the nuclear bomb may make them apprehensive, they prefer to suppress these anxieties, discount the future excessively, and hope for the best. The result is a massive inertia. Though the old ways will not do, the old ways have a terrible momentum even if they are on the wane. Caught on a small and increasingly constricted planet, the nations remain divided. The leaders and their followers are unable to shed old habits and renounce obsolete interests fast enough to ensure themselves and each other a decent chance of survival. The only hope is that the prudence instilled by fear, and luck, will last long enough for a new generation to appear that, intolerant of an appalling man-made dilemma, and irreverent of their fathers' immobilities, will master the monster of unbridled technology.

INDEX

80-82, 108-12, 134, 167-68; diminished usability, 74-79, 82-87, 89, 108-15, 116, 125, 133-37, 139, 143-46, 153, 168-69, 171-73
  value: 7-16, 20, 80-87, 105, 172-73; changes in, 3-6, 12, 14-16, 34, 36-37, 89-90, 97, 108, 133-37, 144, 174; measurability, 8-9, 36-37, 85-86
military power confrontations: classes of nuclear powers, 121-22, 167-69; lesser versus great powers, 74-79, 116-22, 122-27, 144-45, 165-67; lesser versus lesser powers, 127-33; United States versus Soviet Union, 75-79, 87-101, 102-08, 113, 114-15, 139-143, 165-69. *See also* crisis, international
Mill, James, 42
Mills, C. Wright, 32n
Modelski, George, 21n, 46n, 60n, 86n
"modernization," 52, 62, 69, 147-49, 175. *See also* less developed countries
Morgenstern, Oskar, 105n
Morocco, 28, 128, 132

Napoleon, 73; Napoleonic empire, 39; Napoleonic era, 42. *See also* France
Nasser, Gamal Abdel, 73, 128
nationalism, 29, 34, 39, 42, 149; in the nineteenth century, 21, 73-74, 78
NATO, 131, 154, 157, 161
Nazism, 41, 74. *See also* Germany
neo-colonialism, *see* colonialism
Netherlands, 50
neutralism, neutralist countries, *see* non-alignment

Newman, Joseph, 165n
New York Times, 55n
Nicholas II, Tsar, 43
non-alignment, 131, 151, 154, 161-63, 170-71; and public opinion, 64-65, 67, 72, 76. *See also* alliances
Norway, 50, 67, 74
nuclear armaments, *see* armaments, nuclear
nuclear deterrence, *see* deterrence, nuclear
nuclear guarantees, 120, 156, 161
nuclear proliferation, 118-22, 126-27
nuclear stigma, 123-27, 168
Nuremberg trials, 44

Obermann, Emil, 40n
Östgaard, Einar, 61n
Oganisyan, Y., 36n
Olson, Mancur, Jr., 25n
Organization of African Unity, 132. *See also* regional organizations
Organization of American States, 132. *See also* regional organizations

pacifism, 42. *See also* militarism
Pakistan, 28, 53, 127, 128-29, 132
paralysis of decision, 95, 98, 112, 113, 142. *See also* balance of terror
Parsons, Talcott, 32n
Philippines, 28
Poland, 51, 64
Portugal, 73; dependencies of, 71, 128
power, international, 17-20. *See also* bipolarity; influence, international; military power
power package, 15, 168
propaganda, *see* influence,

Other books published for
The Center of International Studies
Woodrow Wilson School of Public and International
Affairs

Gabriel A. Almond, *The Appeals of Communism*

Gabriel A. Almond and James S. Coleman, editors, *The Politics of the Developing Areas*

Gabriel A. Almond and Sidney Verba, *The Civil Culture: Political Attitudes and Democracy in Five Nations*

Richard J. Barnet and Richard A. Falk, *Security in Disarmament*

Cyril E. Black and Thomas P. Thornton, editors, *Communism and Revolution: The Strategic Uses of Political Violence*

Robert J. C. Butow, *Tojo and the Coming of the War*

Miriam Camps, *Britain and the European Community, 1955-1963*

Bernard C. Cohen, *The Political Process and Foreign Policy: The Making of the Japanese Peace Settlement*

Bernard C. Cohen, *The Press and Foreign Policy*

Charles De Visscher, *Theory and Reality in Public International Law*, translated by P. E. Corbett

Frederick S. Dunn, *Peace-making and the Settlement with Japan*

Herman Kahn, *On Thermonuclear War*

W. W. Kaufmann, editor, *Military Policy and National Security*

Klaus Knorr, *The War Potential of Nations*

Klaus Knorr, editor, NATO *and American Security*

Klaus Knorr and Sidney Verba, editors, *The International System: Theoretical Essays*

Sidney J. Ploss, *Conflict and Decision-making in Soviet Russia*

Lucian W. Pye, *Guerrilla Communism in Malaya*

James N. Rosenau, editor, *International Aspects of Civil Strife*

James N. Rosenau, *National Leadership and Foreign Policy: A Case Study in the Mobilization of Public Support*

Rolf Sannwald and Jacques Stohler, *Economic Integration: Theoretical Assumptions and Consequences of European Unification*. Translated by Herman F. Karreman

Richard L. Sklar, *Nigerian Political Parties: Power in an Emergent African Nation*

Glenn H. Snyder, *Deterrence and Defense*

Harold and Margaret Sprout, *The Ecological Perspective on Human Affairs, With Special Reference to International Politics*

Thomas P. Thornton, *The Third World in Soviet Perspective: Studies by Soviet Writers on the Developing Areas*

Sidney Verba, *Small Groups and Political Behavior: A Study of Leadership*

Karl von Vorys, *Political Development in Pakistan*

Myron Weiner, *Party Politics in India*